DELIVERANCE

A Ministry of Compassion

JOSEF ROUSEK

Edited by
BARBARA KAIN PARKER

Graphic Designer
ANNE THOMPSON

Dedicated to:
Tom and Kathy Griner
Father's Heart International

Your heart to see the power of Christ working miracles is what first brought me to Zambia. Your mentoring and friendship have provided a hands-on school of the supernatural. Without those gospel crusades and all that we have learned together, this book and the fruit it will produce would have never been possible. For this, I am extremely grateful.

CONTENTS

FOREWORD

In 1989, as a Baptist pastor I conducted my first prayer session for deliverance. This happened three weeks after beginning a sermon series on spiritual warfare. In preparation for this series, I had ordered several books on deliverance and spiritual warfare and listened to many tapes but must admit that during that first deliverance I really had no idea what I was doing. There were not many tools to help a Baptist pastor lead someone to freedom in 1989.

I can honestly say I found no book as thorough and concise as Josef Rousek's new book, *Deliverance: A Ministry of Compassion*. It's easy to read and is filled with biblical truth, astonishing stories of actual deliverances in Africa and the United States, as well as both practical and very helpful insights. Josef addresses many of the questions that you might have about deliverance and the biblical concept of demonic influence.

You will find this book an excellent addition to your arsenal for helping to set the captives free.

Dr. Paul L. Cox
Aslan's Place, Apple Valley, CA

PREFACE

Deliverance: A Ministry Of Compassion was birthed out of a deep desire in my heart to see people delivered from the evil assaults of the enemy. Additionally, I hope to equip Christians both to understand the reality of demonic influence, even within the Church, and to know what to do about it.

This book is not intended for young readers because the content can be disturbing. It includes frank discussions of the rights through which the enemy gains access to people, including such topics as sexuality, marriage issues, addictions, occult practices, deception, etc. That said, it is also full of 'glory stories' about how evil has been disabled and vanquished from individual lives. It is a book that delivers hope in the midst of seemingly hopeless situations because Jesus is that hope, and He has already overcome all of the evil that we encounter. Furthermore, He has equipped us to do His work on earth to help people become free.

My prayer is that each reader will approach the subject of deliverance with a willingness for the Holy Spirit to deliver insights into healing that far exceed the words written on these pages.

Josef Rousek

CHAPTER 1
COMING INTO UNDERSTANDING

I t was 1995, and my fifteen-year-old daughter, Hayley, and I had decided to travel on a mission trip to Lusaka, Zambia, with my pastor, Eric Stovesand, and his close friend, evangelist Tom Griner. Our goal was to put on a citywide Holy Spirit Seminar along with a four-night outdoor evangelistic meeting. We rented the Mulungushi, the biggest auditorium in the capital city, advertised on the radio, and put up posters throughout the city; on the day of the event about one thousand people showed up. Tom and Pastor Eric shared and taught about the Holy Spirit and the baptism of the Holy Spirit, and then invited people to come forward to receive the Holy Spirit.

While we prayed, a teenage girl fell down and began to thrash and cry out. Some young adults came up and held her down while praying for her. Though I had been attending church for years, I'd never seen anything like that and was amazed, but at the same time interested to understand what was happening. The young people explained that they had cast a demon out of the girl a few weeks previously, but she had gone back into sin and now the demon had come back with more demons seven times more evil. I thought, Wow! I've read about this in the Bible but didn't expect it to be happening in modern times. I didn't realize that this event was a pivotal moment that would change the direction of my life.

The next week, we set up a stage, sound system and lights in a compound (ghetto) named Mandavu. Tom shared each night about Jesus, and, as we prayed for people, many were saved and some were healed of illnesses; one deaf child began to hear.

I also remember praying with Pastor Eric for a deaf boy who was about nine years old. After some time, Eric left, and as I continued to pray, the boy fell down under the power of the Spirit. I caught him up in my arms and began wandering around, carrying this child who was completely out in the Spirit and thinking, OK, now what do I do? After some time, a man came up and said he knew the parents; he offered to carry the boy home, so I handed him off to the man.

 I learned that God can do powerful things whether the person receiving prayer has faith or not.

I never found out if the boy was healed or not, but it was a wonderful lesson for me because I learned that God can do powerful things whether the person receiving prayer has faith or not. Many people believe that the reason people are healed or filled with the Holy Spirit is because they have faith that God is going to do something, and yes, many times there is a faith component but not always. How much faith can a nine-year-old deaf boy have when receiving prayer? He didn't even know what was going on, except for the fact that a white man who was a complete stranger was putting his hands on him and moving his lips. He had no concept of the Father, the Son or the Spirit, and no idea of the words I was praying. The Holy Spirit just decided to enter him, and so He did.

After returning to Zambia several times with Tom, we decided to start a non-profit ministry with two goals in mind: evangelistic meetings where people could be saved and healed, and helping starving children by bringing them into churches for healthy meals. I had seen children living on the streets and digging through trash in search of food, and the Lord placed a burden upon my heart to help them. In keeping with the Father's passion for His people, we named the organization, Father's Heart International:

A father of the fatherless, a defender of widows, Is God in His holy habitation. God sets the solitary in families; He brings out those who are bound into prosperity; But the rebellious dwell in a dry land. (Psalm 68:5-6)

If you then, being evil, know how to give good gifts to your children, how much more will your Father who is in heaven give good things to those who ask Him! (Matthew 7:11)

Even so it is not the will of your Father who is in heaven that one of these little ones should perish. (Matthew 18:14)

As we kept going back to Zambia over the years, we continued doing outdoor meetings and overseeing the churches where we fed the children. Many times, because of lack of funds in Zambia, only the firstborn boy in the family gets to go to school. Often, the girls stay home, working at such chores as hauling water; or they are sent out on the street to sell popcorn or vegetables, leaving them quite vulnerable to abuse on the streets. The pastors wanted to have a school to teach these children and to feed them, so we said that we would do the best we could to fund them.

 At one point, we were supporting over eighty schools with eighteen thousand meals per month.

We met with the World Food Program, which committed to giving us half of a semi-truck-full of high nutrition porridge every month. We bought a delivery truck and hired a driver to deliver porridge to schools all across Zambia; but because Zambia is about the size of Texas, this was quite a challenge. At one point, we were supporting over eighty schools with eighteen thousand meals per month. Thousands of children have had their nutritional needs met and have been educated because of this program. We have watched year after year as the children also learn about Jesus and receive salvation through the school program of Father's Heart.

Josef giving out Bibles

We were also able to buy a house in a nice neighborhood of Lusaka with a high guard wall around it; we needed a safe place to stay and to park our delivery trucks and cars. When the Lord provided funds for us to buy a semi-truck and trailer in South Africa, we had a driver bring it up to Zambia and park it in our back yard. Then we shipped an ocean container from the U. S. with a stage, lights, sound towers, sound equipment and a large generator to provide power for the equipment. Finally, we set out to preach Christ across Zambia.

CHAPTER 2
EVANGELISTIC MEETINGS

The format for evangelistic meetings is this: Our Zambian crusade manager travels to a chosen city to meet with the members of the pastors' society to determine if they want to have a city-wide crusade using the equipment that we supply. He explains they will need to provide:

- Workers to set up the stage and the deliverance tent
- Help with the worship music and crowd control
- Intercessory prayer before the event
- Workers to carry the people who manifest demons during the alter call to the deliverance tent
- Deliverance prayer ministers to pray over the people carried to the tent

If the pastors want us to come, we set a date and pick a soccer field in the center of a compound (ghetto) so the neighborhood people can hear the event and walk to it.

Father's Heart Africa Crusade, Mazabuka, Zambia

We have found that when you Google the population of a city in Zambia; the number may be off quite a bit because no one knows how many people are really in a Zambian city, so we never can know for sure how many to expect. At one meeting in Mazabuka, Google said the city had thirty thousand people and we thought if one-third showed up it would be a good turnout. The first night fifteen thousand attended, and over the next few nights the crowd swelled to thirty thousand.

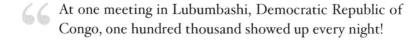
> At one meeting in Lubumbashi, Democratic Republic of Congo, one hundred thousand showed up every night!

The population estimate was obviously wrong because every person in town didn't come. We had a great time singing, dancing and worshipping with thirty thousand people. Many were saved, healed, and delivered of evil spirits.

At one meeting in Lubumbashi, Democratic Republic of Congo, one hundred thousand showed up every night! Other times, only two thousand attended. Sometimes we have many ushers and the crowd is quite organized, but sometimes we are short on ushers and crowd control; when that happens, people are not able to come forward during the alter call because the crowd presses all the way forward to the edge of the stage.

Night after night and year after year, Tom has preached Christ crucified for our sins. Sometimes hundreds come forward to receive Christ; other times we see thousands. Often, we have the crowd pray and ask Jesus to heal them, and there are mass healings. We then bring the healed onto the stage to testify of what the Lord has done. Other times, Tom will ask people who want to be healed to form a line beside the stage and as we begin to pray, many are healed - with some manifesting demons and falling down as in scripture:

> *Now there was a man in their synagogue with an unclean spirit. And he cried out, saying, "Let us alone! What have we to do with You, Jesus of Nazareth? Did You come to destroy us? I know who You are—the Holy One of God!" But Jesus rebuked him, saying, "Be quiet, and come out of him!" And when the unclean spirit had convulsed him and cried out with a loud voice, he came out of him.* (Mark 1:23-26)

During these meetings, I felt like I was in school. Some I prayed for were healed, but most were not. Sometimes people were healed on the spot; other times they received healing during that night while in bed. During one crusade, I prayed for a little girl who was deaf, and her ears were opened. Her friends began to dance and sing for joy. When I asked why they were dancing, they said that their friend could now hear. That same night, Tom and another pastor heard about the girl being healed, so they brought a deaf boy to me to see what would happen; I prayed for him too, but he wasn't healed. The next night though, he returned to the crusade and his ears were open! The Lord had healed him during the night.

One thing that I couldn't understand at first was why many people would manifest demons when I prayed for them. After they came forward in front of the stage, Tom would lead them in a prayer of repentance and a prayer to receive Christ; I would then begin to lay hands on people and pray for them. Over time, I learned that there seemed to be three main types of responses to the spirit realm for those who responded during the altar call and I have learned to recognize what God is doing.

First, are those who come under the power of the Holy Spirit. They have a peaceful appearance; their eyes may be closed but heads are lifted up, and there might be tears of thankfulness rolling down their cheeks. If they are lifting their hands, they may be quivering a bit. When I put my hands on them and ask the Lord to fill them with His Spirit, it happens immediately and many times they begin to speak in other tongues. Sometimes they fall down on the ground under the power of the Spirit. During a meeting we did in Kalomo in 2015, the Holy Spirit began to do something different through me; as I prayed my abdomen would become tight and I could feel a lot of power flowing through my belly, up through my torso, and out my arms and hands. Person after person I prayed for were filled with the Spirit of God and began to speak in new tongues. There seemed to be a discharge of power into each person, and then I would be recharged as I moved to the next. I am thankful that even after all these years of ministry God continues to do wonderful new things in and through me.

 God is always faithful to complete His work in them.

The second group seemed to be like deer in headlights. Their eyes are wide open with no visual evidence of the power of God on them. In such cases, they might have come forward simply out of curiosity, and they seem too connected to the world. But just because I can see nothing happening outwardly doesn't mean nothing is happening inside. These people have come forward and prayed to receive Christ, so something is probably happening in the Spirit, for no one can come to Christ unless God draws that one to Himself. [1]Or, some might not have their heart in the correct place; they could be just going through the motions without a sincere desire to know Jesus. Many times I have prayed for this type of person and have not seen the Lord move in power upon them, but because time is short during an altar call, maybe only thirty minutes or less, I do look to see what God is doing and try to participate with what I can discern. Though I no longer spend much time praying for these people, I can rest assured that if their decision is sincere, God is always faithful to complete His work in them. [2]

The third group is those who are manifesting evil. When people come forward and encounter the power of the Holy Spirit that is around the stage, demons begin to manifest. It can be quite as simple as the person crying out and falling down, shaking and writhing as the demon asserts control over the person's physical body. The ushers carry these people to the deliverance tent because they are quite disruptive, and we cannot pray for healing and the baptism of the Holy Spirit for others in the midst of people manifesting and thrashing around. It is also dangerous to the new believers and prayer ministers, so out of courtesy and respect for all, we need to get the person that is manifesting out of the dirt and into a safe clean environment. There is a vinyl floor in our tent that provides a clean and more private place where they can receive further prayer; we cover the women with a cloth to maintain their dignity.

Some that come forward to receive Christ may look like they are receiving the baptism of the Spirit, but in reality, a demon is faking it. Demons are not dumb, and I believe they may do that so that I will not lay my hands on them as I walk by. They must know that if someone is getting baptized in the Spirit, then I will just let the Holy Spirit do His ministry and leave the person without prayer. Evil spirits know what the baptism of the Holy Spirit looks like and will fake it so that I will stay away from them. They are afraid of the authority of God that I carry and don't want me to me to be near them or to cast them out.

They have a demonic tongue that they often cause the person to speak, perhaps hoping I will walk by and think to myself, "That person is doing fine; they are speaking in tongues and are getting baptized in the Spirit. " It took me a few years to understand this, but now I can listen to the tongue and discern if it is evil or if it is from the Lord. Unfortunately, I have heard this demonic tongue spoken in churches in the United States as well. It doesn't flow out like a holy tongue; it is choppy and repetitive and sounds quite different. Now I don't even need to use spiritual discernment to identify this tongue because it is very distinct and different than a tongue of the Spirit or a tongue of angels.

This type of person usually falls down and manifests when I pray for them. Their eyelids may start to flicker softly before they fall, and sometimes their eyes roll up so only the whites of the eyes show, but often the eyelids remain closed. Sometimes trying to understand in the Spirit what is happening, I will lift up their eyelid with my thumb and I will see that their eyes are rolled up and only the white of their eyes is showing, which means there is a demon present. I pray and command, "Unclean spirit, I bind you in the name of Jesus. You must leave now. " These people are then taken to the deliverance tent for further prayer.

During a crusade in Victoria Falls, Zimbabwe, in 2017, I observed something I have never seen before. A woman who came forward to receive the baptism of the Holy Spirit began to speak loudly in a holy tongue, with tears running down her cheeks. After about thirty seconds, she switched to a demonic tongue and continued to switch back and forth from one to the other. I addressed the Zimbabwean pastor that was standing next to me, "Listen to this. " Excited to see something new, something I had never seen before, I wanted to share it with him and also was wondering if he could understand the difference. He replied, "There seems to be a mixture. " He could understand what was happening, so I was pleased. I then spoke into her ear, "Unclean spirit, I bind you in the name of Jesus. You must leave now. " I took her by the hand as she continued speaking loudly in both tongues and guided her to stand in the corner of the deliverance tent while I began casting some demons out of others who were manifesting. After about fifteen minutes, she began speaking only in a holy tongue; I was listening, thanking God that He had delivered her. After another fifteen minutes of speaking the holy tongue, she stopped, and I asked her how she felt. She replied, "Good. " I then said, "You got a good dose of the Spirit tonight," and her reply was a big, beautiful smile. The Holy Spirit had regenerated her spirit, and she now had the mind of Christ; Holy Spirit had come in, and her body had become His temple. No one, no evil spirit, can now snatch her from the hand of God. After a power encounter with the Holy Spirit like that, there is no going back to the old. When I see her in heaven, I will enjoy seeing that smile again!

There are many ways a person can manifest a demon. At the second evangelistic meeting I attended in Zambia, a woman came up on the stage for prayer. As Tom prayed for her, she fell back and manifested. Following Jesus' example, he asked how many demons there were and what their names were. [3] There were three that gave their names and he told them to leave; it looked like they did and the woman got up and was in her right mind, so Tom led her in a prayer to receive Christ. The next night he asked the crowd if the lady who had been delivered of evil spirits the night before was there. She was, and I helped her up the stairs and onto the stage; Tom asked how she was doing and she explained in very good English that for years she had been forced by these demons to take off her clothes and walk naked through the streets at night. She didn't like leaving her children at home alone, and the only way she could appease the demons was to drink chicken blood. The previous night had been the first time in many years that she stayed in bed and slept well. She said she was now free!

Later, when it was time to pray for the people that had come forward, I watched to see what the Holy Spirit was doing, and He highlighted a woman in the front row, so I began to walk toward her. When I got about ten feet away, demonic power picked her up off the ground about three feet and she quickly flew about forty feet back into the crowd, knocking several people down. When she landed, she began to writhe and scream as a demon manifested. I thought to myself, "Wow, what am I carrying that would cause that?" People levitating and flying is so bizarre, but here it was happening right before me. I was beginning to step into the spiritual realms where things occur that one wouldn't believe possible.

Another time, my daughter Hayley traveled with me to Zambia. During an altar call, we were praying for people when Hayley came over to show me something. She had been laying her hand, palm open, on a woman's abdomen while praying for healing of the stomach where there was a lump that could be felt on the outside, but when she put her hand on the lump and prayed, it would move. Once I confirmed the lump was moving around, we knew a demon was in there, so we asked Jesus to remove it and the woman was completely healed of stomach problems.

While ministering once in Mongu, Zambia, an older woman from a village who was dressed in a traditional wrap skirt (Shetangi) and a head wrap (Shetamballa) asked for prayer. Fortunately, she was standing in sand, because as we prayed, she fell down onto her back. Realizing it was a demonic manifestation, we commanded it to come out. The woman then began to slither through the sand away from us with the same movement as a snake. I stood in amazement for a moment because the human skeleton is unable to normally flex enough to move like a snake, but somehow evil was manipulating her bones to flex supernaturally so that she could propel herself along just like a snake. We followed her, commanding the snake demon to leave, which it did after a few minutes. The woman stood up and was in her right mind. I remember thinking that I'd better keep this to myself because nobody back home was going to believe it.

Another time, in Mazabuka, a woman who responded to the altar call fell down manifesting a demon and was carried to our deliverance tent by the ushers. When they laid her down on the floor, she jumped up and began dancing like a prizefighter—leading with her left fist, bouncing, punching, bobbing, and counter punching. I thought I had seen it all, but this woman must have picked up a demonic spirit that had been in a professional fighter; it was the only way she could have learned to move like this. It is possible that there was a boxing spirit that may have come out of a fighter when he died, later entered the woman, and was now manifesting in such a strange way. That same night, another woman who was a witch doctor (Nanga) was manifesting in the deliverance tent. When my wife, Anne, walked in, the woman sat up and locked eyes with her. The appearance of the woman's eyes changed from human to demonic and she tried to put Anne into a trance. I took my wife by the arm and said, "It's time to leave now." There were other prayer ministers to pray for the witch.

Anne and I have continued to travel to Zambia with Tom and Kathy Griner for the past twenty years; we still do outdoor evangelism, praying for the sick, casting out demons and praying for the baptism of the Holy Spirit to come upon the people who respond. On a normal night, fifty to one hundred people will manifest demons, so you can imagine how many more deliverance stories we have to tell!

CHAPTER 3
SELF WILL

When I first began doing evangelistic meetings, I wondered how people with demons could come forward to receive Christ. Didn't the demons possess and control them? The demons know that there is power to drive them out up near the stage, but the people still come forward. It is clear that demons can't stand that overwhelming presence of the Holy Spirit; so much so that the tormented individual is thrown to the ground and begins screaming. Obviously, the demon is not having a good day, so why did it let the person walk up into the danger zone? So many questions came to mind.

Watching the crowd during the altar call, it is clear that some people remain where they are and don't respond. Why? Some are already saved. Some don't want Jesus. Some simply walk away and head home. Many don't come forward because the evil spirits affect their thinking and they are blinded to the truth.

> *...whose minds the god of this age has blinded, who do not believe, lest the light of the gospel of the glory of Christ, who is the image of God, should shine on them. (2 Corinthians 4:4)*

It is interesting when some people who do come forward to receive Christ also manifest a demon. Why do the demons allow a response to the altar call? It's because a person's self-will is powerful and can overcome the demonic control. The demon may be doing everything it knows to stay in the host, trying to prevent them from receiving Christ, but the person's self-will says, "I am going forward; I want this Jesus. " This self-will is a powerful gift that the Lord has given us to help lead us to salvation and deliverance.

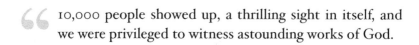

> 10,000 people showed up, a thrilling sight in itself, and we were privileged to witness astounding works of God.

Over the years, I learned that many people can actually have evil spirits inside them, just as the Bible teaches, and that the power given to us through Jesus is fully able to drive them out. For the first ten years or so, during the evangelistic meetings in Zambia, some would be healed, some would get baptized in the Spirit, and some would manifest demons. When I would tell the demon to come out, it rarely did, and the person would just keep manifesting. Our American ministry team would leave the crusade and head back to the hotel while the African prayer ministers would stay behind and finish the work of deliverance. I often wondered why the demons didn't always come out when I told them to, and I suspected that all who were carried to the tent didn't get delivered, even though the deliverance team would report that they all did. Most did, perhaps, but I wondered if some demons might have just released physical control of the person, retreating back into the mind or body and hiding out of sight of the prayer ministers, deceiving them into believing the deliverance had been accomplished.

Things shifted during an evangelistic meeting in Nakonde, Zambia, in 2010. It was a wonderful meeting, with the stage set up on a small hill near the city center. The panoramic view was fantastic, and in the evening huge thunderheads built up in the distance. The view out into Tanzania was especially incredible because the land was so flat you could actually see the curvature of the earth on the horizon. The population of Nakonde was 20,000, and on the first night 10,000 people showed up, a thrilling sight in itself, and we were privileged to witness astounding works of God.

A crippled woman was carried to the meeting and lifted onto the stage. Tom prayed for her, and when she was lifted to her feet she began to walk. She remained in a chair onstage to rest for a while, but when the keyboard player began to play, she stood up and started dancing! We were all elated.

A man with a blind eye that looked off to one side was in the crowd a few rows back from the front. We could see that the man was really reaching out to the Lord for healing, so Tom asked me to go into the crowd and lay hands on him. The crowd was packed so tight against the stage that I could not get to him, and Tom prayed for his healing from a distance. It didn't look like anything was happening, so Tom moved on to minister to others. However, after fifteen minutes, the man with the crooked blind eye worked his way to the front and came up the stairs. I asked why he had come forward, because his eye was still messed up and looking off to the side. He explained that he was healed and that he could see. I thought to myself, "OK, whom am I to doubt his healing, but it is not really looking very healed!" We gave him the microphone and he told the crowd he could see. Tom held up some fingers and the man covered his good eye; with the crooked eye he could see how many fingers Tom displayed. The next day, as Tom was in line to cross the border into Tanzania, a man came up and asked, "Do you remember me? I am the man with the blind eye. " His eye was now clear and looking straight ahead! During the night Jesus had healed his eye and straightened it out; the Holy Spirit is a healer!

During that same meeting, I spent some time in the deliverance tent where I encountered a girl who was about sixteen years old. She was rolling around on the floor, manifesting a demon. Prayer ministers were yelling, "Come out!" over and over but there was no change. The demons kept trying to tear off her shirt, but the ministers would hold her arms to stop her; this went on for 45 minutes. I asked the ministry team why she couldn't get free, and they explained that her grandmother was a witch doctor and had done some powerful witchcraft on her. Then the girl came to her right mind and said that she needed to relieve herself. She stood up and, with a female prayer minister holding each arm, calmly walked toward the woods. I thought, "Wow, what happened to the demon? It was obviously still there but it stopped acting out. Surely it could have regained control of the girl, caused her to pull her arms free of the deliverance ministers and run away, but it didn't. It seemed so odd that it controlled the girl for a time and then it just stopped and the girl regained her senses. As I drove the long twelve hours back to our house in Lusaka, I wondered how this stuff works. I had a simple theology that the demons that came out couldn't go into me because I was a Christian and where there was light there could be no darkness, but a holy hunger to understand what was happening set in.

CHAPTER 4
THE LIGHT COMES ON

After returning to the states I called my friend, Pastor Eric, and asked, "Can a Christian have a demon?" He said that he did believe that could happen and suggested I phone our mutual friend, Anna, because she knew more about it and could answer my questions. We'd all been together on a mission trip to Russia when it first opened to westerners about ten years before, and I was still occasionally in contact with her.

When Anna answered I asked, "Can a Christian have a demon?" Anna replied, "Of course a Christian can have a demon. " Quite polite and able to come down to my basic level of understanding, she answered my questions and then recommended a book by Derek Prince, *They Shall Expel Demons.*

https://www.amazon.com/dp/0800792602

I ordered it in paperback along with the audio CD. My wife Anne was in my office when I opened the box. She asked me if she could have the CD and I said that I was planning on listening to it on the way home. She was adamant, so I gave her the audio book. At the time I was wondering why she wanted it so badly—it was quite surprising because she had never been interested in ministering deliverance before. As we look back now, we can see that the Lord was birthing a desire to learn in both of us at the same time. I began to read the book while she listened to the audio book. After finishing the book, I was walking in a meadow near my house and sat down on a rock. I decided to try self-deliverance just to see what would happen and said out loud, "In the name of Jesus, evil spirits come out. " As soon as I finished speaking, I coughed a couple of times, and knew immediately that I coughed out some demons. Surprised, I thought, "Oh wow, I do have some!"

That same week Anne was in a hotel in San Diego, having listened to the audio book on the long drive down. She woke up in the morning and was reading the Bible when she began to feel strange. She looked up, and the Lord opened her eyes to see into the spiritual realm. To her surprise, there were two hideous-looking demons hovering in the corner of her room. She commanded them to leave and they went outside where she could see them floating through the window, blocked from re-entering by a large white dove with its wings wide-spread. As you can imagine, it was quite upsetting to her.

The following week we were together at home, getting suited up for a bicycle ride. She told me about her experience in the hotel room, and I shared what had happened to me. It was a strange moment for both of us to realize that she had demons around her, and I had demons coming out of me. We looked into each other's eyes with excitement that God was moving in our lives. We often ride separately because Anne is stronger and faster than me, so I got on my bike and went south while she rode north. I descended Rock Creek Canyon and turned around for the climb back up when a heavy anointing of the Holy Spirit came upon me. I clicked one foot out of my cleats and put my foot on the ground. An open vision of images of people that I knew flashed quickly in front of my eyes; there were many and the Lord was moving them by so quickly that I began to laugh because it was like He'd plugged a broadband cable into my head. There was so much revelation happening so fast and so much anointing that I said out loud, "Lord, fire wire!" I knew that the people he was showing me were Christians that needed deliverance, It was one of the most powerful spiritual experiences I have ever had.

Over the next few days there was a shift in my thinking about spiritual things, and since that experience I have never been the same because He opened up an understanding of how the spirit world operates. I began to notice evil spirits operating in people as I went through my day; sometimes they would even speak to me through people in public places. I had heard stories about this kind of thing from Pastor Albie Pearson, but I never expected it to start happening to me.

Nevertheless, do not rejoice in this, that the spirits are subject to you, but rather rejoice because your names are written in heaven. In that hour Jesus rejoiced in the Spirit and said, "I thank You, Father, Lord of heaven and earth, that You have hidden these things from the wise and prudent and revealed them to babes. (Luke 10:20-21)

I continued to call Anna to ask questions about deliverance, and eventually shared that I fight depression, which had begun during my twenties when I lived for several months each year in Yosemite Valley to go rock climbing. One day my friend and I were rapping off (sliding down the rope) a vertical route that we had finished climbing. On the last rap we threaded the rope through a sling tied to a tree branch and I started sliding toward the ground. When I got to the end of the rope, I could see that I was still twenty-five feet off the ground and realized that the branch wasn't the correct rappel anchor; I should have threaded the rope through a sling more to the right. One side of the rope was longer than the other because I had never marked the center. I yelled up to my friend that I was going to stand on a small foothold and slide the rope through my rappel device so I could get the ends of the rope even. That maneuver would at least allow me to get a few feet closer to the ground. While I was sliding the rope, my foot slipped off the hold and one end of the rope slid through the rappel device. I began to free fall, hitting the ground on my feet but falling backward very hard. I didn't pass out but was quite disoriented. My landing was in a boulder field, but by the grace of God I landed between the boulders; otherwise I could have split my skull open on a rock as I fell back.

I was quite shaken, and decided to leave the Valley to recover, but over the next few weeks I sunk into a deep depression. I went home to stay with my parents and just felt like crying all the time; the feeling of depression was debilitating. My father sent me to see a psychiatrist who diagnosed me with depression. Back then, since the drugs we have today were not available, treatment was limited to lithium and/or electroshock therapy, neither of which was an option. The doctor asked me if I had a girlfriend and I answered, "No. " He said, "Why not?" My response, "I don't know, I just don't have one. " He recommended that I get a girlfriend and sleep with her, which I didn't do because I wasn't very good at meeting girls. Over time the depression diminished but it would come and go, never getting back to the original intensity, but still present for many years. There might be a few weeks of feeling normal but then a few days of mild-to-moderate depression would set in.

 I have been free of depression for seven years.

While talking with Anna on the phone, she suggested that a demon was causing the depression and asked if I wanted her to cast it out. I was home alone and asked, "Will I manifest?" She answered that I wouldn't, so I laid down on our couch and said, "Go ahead and pray. " In a calm voice she prayed something simple like this, "Spirit of anxiety, leave Joe now. " I didn't feel anything leave; I didn't feel any deliverance; so, I told her thanks and hung up the phone. But I did feel better and wasn't depressed, so I thought, "OK, let's see if anything happens. " Over the next few weeks I waited to see if I was healed or if the depression would come back. Several times it would try to creep back in but I would either say in my mind or speak out loud, "You are not coming back in," and it would leave. As of this writing, I have been free of depression for seven years. Those who know what depression feels like can relate to how wonderful it is to live without it. I am very thankful that Jesus is my deliverer.

Based on some reading about deliverance, I've learned that people can pick up demons during times of disorientation or unconsciousness, such as that which results from the impact of car accidents or general anesthesia during surgery. Many people teach that personal or generational sin is what gives a demon the legal right to enter a person and that is generally true, but not always. I believe that when I hit the ground in the climbing accident and became so disoriented, an evil spirit of depression entered me and stayed for years until someone with authority confronted it, at which point it left easily with no outward signs of leaving. During deliverance ministry sessions you don't need to see anything happen outwardly to know that your prayers are working; many times there is no noticeable sign that the evil spirit is leaving and over time it becomes clear if there was deliverance or not through the person's experience. Often, the gift of discernment may allow one to feel the deliverance and know immediately that something is happening, but I'll get to more about that later.

I continued calling Anna with hundreds of questions; she was an extremely knowledgeable and patient teacher, faithfully answering all of them. I learned that multiple demons often work together, and when one comes into a person, it opens the door to let others in. It is generally incorrect to say a person has a demon when in reality it's a whole team at work, so it is more appropriate to say that someone is demonized. That may sound a bit heavy but really just means demons are affecting how they think and/or act. Anna continued to minister to me, and over time she cast several more demons out.

I asked Anna to come to Crowley Lake to teach Anne and me how to minister deliverance to people. I set up several ministry sessions, during the second one I had a vivid vision of what happened many generations back that allowed a curse to come into a woman's bloodline. I was quite surprised that God would show me such a clear vision to help in the ministry! Then we continued doing sessions with my wife and I being physically with a person while Anna led the session over Skype. Learning how to help people get free was quite exciting.

When I would return to the US from Africa, I would often wonder why people didn't seem to manifest in the same way here, but then a Christian woman in Nevada manifested when we prayed for her. I thought, "Finally, I have seen someone in the U. S. manifest after seeing thousands manifest in Zambia." I knew that evil spirits would also be in people in the U. S. ; it just made sense, but I had to wait twelve years to see it happen. A few months later I was in a church and the lady who had manifested was also there. She asked the pastor for the microphone so she could testify and said that she had been on anti-depressants, but the Lord had healed her, and she was now medication free!

Another close friend asked for prayer, so my wife Anne and I prayed for her. She was both bi-polar and gluten intolerant. The bi-polar issue was in the generational line on her mom's side and continued back to her grandmother and then to her great grand-mother. We led her in a prayer to break the generational rights and then told some specific evil spirits to leave. The next day I called to see how she was doing, and she replied that she'd gone home and eaten a large pizza. I asked why she didn't eat just one piece to see what would happen and she said that she knew that she was healed so she just kept eating. I am still in contact with her and she is still free not only of the gluten intolerance but also the bi-polar disease.

Anna asked if my wife and I would like to go to Hesperia, California, to get some generational deliverance from her friend Dr. Paul Cox. I watched a video on his web site, and it looked kind of kooky - way out of my comfort zone! I asked Anna if what Paul was doing was biblical, and she replied that she had been there many times and it was very biblical. My wife and I agreed to get ministry there, splitting a three-hour session.

We came for a morning session. Paul was there, along with Anna and several of Paul's interns. I wanted to get ministry first, but Paul asked the Lord who should go first and discerned it was to be Anne. He had her read some prayers out of a book and did some ministry for a couple of hours. Then I read some prayers and had some ministry too. After the session, while driving to Las Vegas and working a trade show for my job, I remember how free I felt; it was as if I was walking a foot off the ground. There was so much peace, more than I had ever felt in my life.

. . .

I booked another appointment with Paul Cox a month later, this time with a full three hours for myself. I read all the prayers he asked me to, and he cast some demons out; but when I left it felt like my mind wasn't working correctly, as if there was a dull fog in my mind. It is hard to put into words, but what I believe was happening is that when the evil that was in my mind left, it took some time for my mind to redirect and to correctly use those areas that had been controlled. It felt like my mind was discovering new neural pathways that it couldn't access before, and it took about three weeks for this feeling to reside. A friend who had a session with Paul the day after I did say she also had experienced the same sensation for about three weeks.

The ministry of Paul and Donna Cox is named Aslan's Place and is located in Apple Valley, CA. In those days, they offered an internship program that taught how to minister using his generational model. It was perfect for me because I could move at my own pace. After the initial five-day school I could read the books, watch the videos and turn in the assignments with no set deadline, graduating when I finished the work. It took me about one and one-half years to complete and then pass a final test, which was to do a prayer ministry session while Paul watched. During that session it was hard to figure out how to pray, and it felt like I had to pull the information out with specific questions so I could know what to do next. Eventually though, the Lord showed me what to pray for, and I began to discern the deliverance. Then I knew I was passing the test. Paul didn't say anything during the session, but after about forty-five minutes he said, "OK you have passed!"

We have appreciated Aslan's Place so much that even though it is a four-hour drive from home, we continue to go. I really enjoy the meetings there and attend often. I also sit in with Paul during deliverance sessions when possible so I can continue to learn more about discernment. Needless to say, I highly recommend Aslan's Place for those who feel they need deliverance or want to learn how to minister deliverance!

One of the discernment gifts that God has given many people is the ability to see the spirit realm, which surrounds us and is very real, as real as the natural realm, in fact. Just because most people can't see it, doesn't make it false, but many pastors just don't know what to do with seers. They don't understand, so they label it as too subjective and not worth paying attention to. They might believe what a prophet says about individuals, but the seer's testimony is too incredible for them to believe. Actually the seer gifting is a wonderful, God-given discernment tool that is very useful in helping people become free. Seers might not be up in front of the church proclaiming individual prophecy, but they are just as gifted and extremely helpful in understanding what is happing within the spiritual atmosphere.

A favorite biblical example of seeing into the spirit realm is:

And Elisha prayed, and said, "Lord, I pray, open his eyes that he may see." Then the Lord opened the eyes of the young man, and he saw. And behold, the mountain was full of horses and chariots of fire all around Elisha. (2 Kings 6:17 NIV)

The horses and chariots of fire were real, but the young man could not see them until the Lord opened his eyes. Several people I know have had their eyes opened to see into the spirit realms, and often they have been doing so since they were small children. My wife, Anne, is a gifted seer and I believe her when she describes something that she is seeing. For me it is not, "Well maybe, that is so subjective," because I know she sees very clearly and that is what is really happing in the spirit realm.

I listened to an excellent audible book on seeing called *The Vail*, written by Blake Healy, and recommend it to anyone that is interested in understanding how 'seeing' works. I don't agree one hundred percent with Blake's doctrine, but it is very interesting to hear about what he sees going on in the atmosphere. The detail he sees is amazing.

During a deliverance session, the goal is to get as much deliverance accomplished as you can so understanding what is going on spiritually is vital. The gifts of seeing, compassion, discernment, and healing, along with the ability to hear from God, are all of vital importance to help us understand how to minister; without God's help we can do nothing but try to console the person.

My gifting is primarily the prophetic, not as one holding the office of a prophet, but still primarily prophetic. I can see in the spirit a little bit and mainly operate through visions, along with other types of discernment. In one session, I knew that there was a hangman's noose around the woman's neck but couldn't see it; I just knew it was there. Knowing is a form of discernment. I could then feel that it was there with my hand. I also knew that the woman was surrounded by twenty-four unrighteous elders, and I could discern them with my hand but could not see them. Up to now, I minister with a different gifting than a seer, and I believe the Lord will continue to increase my giftings as He pleases throughout the rest of my life. That is how it has been so far, so why would He stop?

I do prefer to minister with a seer so I can gather more information. The more you understand, the more you can break off, cast out and disconnect from the person. I would not say that a seer is more effective in deliverance than a person with other discernments, but it is always useful is to combine the gifts of one or more prayer ministers whenever possible. This way you get as much deliverance as you can during the time allotted to the session.

CHAPTER 5
THE MISSION OF JESUS

During his public ministry years, deliverance was one of the main things Jesus did. Today, the American church loves Jesus' commandment to heal the sick, and if we had any lepers around, the church would gladly pray for them. Christians might even pray for the dead. However, when it comes to casting out demons, the church generally doesn't want to get into all that messy stuff. Many churches don't even believe that a Christian can *have* a demon. If they do believe it, their logic often goes something like this, "It would be offensive to cast a demon out of someone, because if you insinuated that they had a demon in the first place it would be rude; and we don't want to be rude. We can't take the chance of offending anyone, because we are Christians and we need to be nice or they might not come back to our church." This type of logic is not Christ-like; it does not show His love. We are commanded in scripture to cast out demons, and if we want to follow Jesus' teachings, we need to cast out demons!

Heal the sick, cleanse the lepers, raise the dead, cast out demons. Freely you have received, freely give. (Matthew 10:8)

Then they went into Capernaum, and immediately on the Sabbath He entered the synagogue and taught. And they were astonished at His teaching, for He taught them as one having authority, and not as the scribes. Now there was a man in their synagogue with an unclean spirit. And he cried out, saying, "Let us alone! What have we to do with You, Jesus of Nazareth? Did You come to destroy us? I know who You are— the Holy One of God!" But Jesus rebuked him, saying, "Be quiet, and come out of him!" And when the unclean spirit had convulsed him and cried out with a loud voice, he came out of him. (Mark 1:21-26)

It is interesting that the events in the above scripture happened in a public place with people watching. The demon spoke to Jesus first in a plural tense, followed by a singular, *"Let us alone...I know who you are."* Jesus responded directly to the demons, *"Be quiet, and come out of him!"* Even though Jesus knew that the man might manifest it and could be embarrassing, He decided to cast it out on the spot. It would be reasonable to think that the man was a member of the synagogue and it could have been an uncomfortable situation for him, but Jesus understood that helping the man become free was the primary issue. *And when the unclean spirit had convulsed him and cried out with a loud voice, he came out of him.* Clearly, Jesus felt it was quite acceptable to do deliverance in both the synagogue and public places. The time for the deliverance was now; this is what the Father was doing, and Jesus understood the importance of God's perfect timing and only did what Father God was leading Him to do. When the demons cried out and spoke to Him, then it was time to tell them to leave. It was fine to allow the man to manifest in public, and the end result of his freedom was the compassionate thing to do.

> Jesus understood the importance of God's perfect timing and only did what Father God was leading Him to do.

At one home meeting, my wife and I were sharing about how the Lord had been setting us free from demons. When I finished, the Lord gave me a prophetic word for a woman attendee that she would move in deliverance ministry. I thought that the word was about some distant time in the future but right after I delivered the word, a woman next to her began to manifest a demon. She sounded like she was vomiting, but no liquid was coming out. The first woman turned to the second woman and said, "In the name of Jesus come out!" To my amazement, the prophetic word was fulfilled right before our eyes. Just as Jesus had done, we allowed the deliverance to take place in public. To try to escort the afflicted woman to another room would have been more disruptive than just getting the job done on the spot. When something like that happens in a small group, the meeting changes to a deliverance meeting. As Jesus did in the synagogue, so we also need to allow the deliverance to be accomplished right there. The Holy Spirit started it, and He knows what time and place is right. There's no need to be ashamed. It really should be a joyful occasion, for the power of God has come to set someone free from evil. It certainly is a time to rejoice for me!

Jesus preached about the Kingdom of God, healed people and cast out demons; it was an important part of His ministry:

On that very day some Pharisees came, saying to Him, "Get out and depart from here, for Herod wants to kill You." And He said to them, "Go, tell that fox, Behold, I cast out demons and perform cures today and tomorrow, and the third day I shall be perfected." (Luke 13:31)

Then one of the crowd answered and said, "Teacher, I brought You my son, who has a mute spirit. And wherever it seizes him, it throws him down; he foams at the mouth, gnashes his teeth, and becomes rigid. So I spoke to Your disciples, that they should cast it out, but they could not." He answered him and said, "O faithless generation, how long shall I be with you? How long shall I bear with you? Bring him to Me." Then they brought him to Him. And when he saw Him, immediately the spirit convulsed him, and he fell on the ground and wallowed, foaming at the mouth. So He asked his father, "How long has this been happening to him?" And he said, "From childhood." And often he has thrown him both into the fire and into the water to destroy him. But if You can do anything, have compassion on us and help us." Jesus said to him, "If you can believe, all things are possible to him who believes." Immediately

the father of the child cried out and said with tears, "Lord, I believe;
help my unbelief!" When Jesus saw that the people came running
together, He rebuked the unclean spirit, saying to it: "Deaf and dumb
spirit, I command you, come out of him and enter him no more!" Then
the spirit cried out, convulsed him greatly, and came out of him. And he
became as one dead, so that many said, "He is dead." But Jesus took him
by the hand and lifted him up, and he arose. And when He had come
into the house, His disciples asked Him privately, "Why could we not
cast it out? So He said to them, "This kind can come out by nothing but
prayer and fasting." (Mark 9:17-28)

Once again, Jesus did the deliverance in public. This scripture illustrates that there is an unclean spirit that causes deafness and dumb-
ness; often, when one is unable to hear sound they also cannot speak
and are mute. In this case, the boy also manifested whenever he was
close to fire or water because the unclean spirit wanted to cause even
further destruction by burning or drowning him. This spirit had been
in the boy since childhood; it might have even been there from birth
due to a right obtained from generational sin. Jesus identified it as a
deaf and dumb spirit, commanded it to come out and enter him no
more. Clearly, Jesus knew it wasn't enough for it to just come out, so
He told it not to return. In response, the spirit cried out and convulsed
the boy, which didn't seem to bother Jesus at all. He knew this was
going to happen, so even though the boy appeared to be dead He
wasn't worried and calmly took his hand and helped him up. The time
for the deliverance was now, not later in a private session where the
father and son would both be sparred any embarrassment. This is a
great model for prayer ministers.

On a recent trip to Zambia, we had four people come on stage for
healing prayer, one of whom was deaf and dumb. Pastor Keith
Kepembwe put a finger in each of his ears and said, "In the name of
Jesus, deaf and dumb spirit come out!"He pulled his fingers away and
the unclean spirit left. Immediately, a smile came on the man's face and
I knew he was healed—we have seen the deaf healed many times. This
man was very excited and we tried to get him to say "Jesus," but he
hadn't learned how to make words yet so he couldn't quite get it right;

but that didn't matter because the important thing was he had been deaf and dumb but now Jesus had healed him.

In the passage above, the disciples came to Jesus in private asking why they could not cast it out. Jesus answered, *This kind can come out by nothing but prayer and fasting.* I believe He was teaching them that prayer and fasting increases the authority that a prayer minister has over this kind of spirit. A friend of mine fasts and prays for three days before ministering to someone with a deaf and dumb spirit.

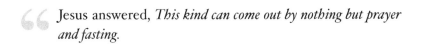

Jesus answered, *This kind can come out by nothing but prayer and fasting.*

A missionary friend of mine who does ministry in Zimbabwe is a wonderful lady who loves Africa. Over seventy years old, she spends months there each year, staying and traveling with a Zimbabwean friend while ministering to the rural poor. She had been medically treating a village woman with a severely burned leg, which had happened because whenever she approached a fire, she would have an epileptic seizure and then would fall into it. She had been burned many times. I reminded my missionary friend about Mark 9 and encouraged her to consider the spiritual cause of the natural effect; yes, medically treating a woman with a burned leg is wonderfully compassionate, but how much better to go a step farther and cast out the unclean spirit. She explained that she was afraid it would not leave, so I encouraged her to just try to cast out the demon the next time she sees the woman. If it doesn't work, at least she will have tried. I suspect that my friend has much more authority over evil than she realizes. But isn't that often the case with many of us? How often do we move by faith in the power of Jesus as He told us to do rather than fearing what might or might not happen? Probably not enough.

Some of my personal guidelines for more effective ministry in my local area include:

- I prefer to make an appointment with someone for prayer ministry rather than do it after a church service because that way I can take my time to go deeper and get more deliverance for the person.

- If I am praying for someone after church and they manifest, I cast out the evil spirit because that is what the Holy Spirit is doing at the moment. I might never see the person again, so if I am going to help them through prayer, it will have to be on the spot.

- If I have prayed for someone after church, I encourage them to come in for more prayer because there is always more deliverance available. Just because a few evil spirits leave doesn't mean a person is totally free, and there are probably more evil spirits with generational rights that need to be broken. Some people take up my offer, while others don't .

- If someone shares something that they would like prayer for, I immediately try to set up an appointment. I have found that otherwise the moment might be lost if evil asserts itself, convincing them that they are fine and that it is just their flesh that is the problem.

- During an appointment, my wife and I can interview the person and see what the Holy Spirit shows us. That results in more deliverance for the individual than is possible in a public meeting.

I imagine Jesus probably spent a lot of one-on-one time with His disciples, ministering deliverance to them. For them to complete the mission that the Father had for them, they would need to be cleaned up and free from evil influence.

When the sun had set, they brought to Him all who were sick and those who were demon-possessed. And the whole city was gathered together at the door. Then He healed many who were sick with various diseases, and cast out many demons; and He did not allow the demons to speak, because they knew Him. (Mark 32:3)

This passage reminds me what ministering outdoors during the evening in Zambia is like. Many come believing they need healing, when in reality they need deliverance most of the time.

Yes, of course, there is a time to pray for healing. An older woman who had been hit by a car months before, came to our meeting in Chawama, Zambia. As a result, she was blind in one eye and her arm was deformed because a fracture had not been set correctly. Someone on our team prayed for healing and the Lord healed both the eye and the arm at the same time.

Another time, during a crusade in Kalomo, five men carried a paralyzed man up to the front of the stage and laid him on a blanket, face down. I thought that we would pray for healing and wondering if I had enough faith, but Pastor Keith had a word from the Lord to pray for deliverance. Specific prayer gets the best results, and we could have prayed for healing and the Lord might have done it, but with the word from the Lord, Keith commanded the demon to come out and the man began to moan. Within minutes the demons that were causing the paralysis left, and he was standing up and walking around. His wife was quite elated, and so was the whole ministry team! In Mark 9, Jesus didn't pray for the boy with epilepsy to be healed; instead he prayed more accurately in accordance with what He knew the Spirit was doing and told the deaf and dumb spirits to leave.

When Jesus sent out the twelve disciples, He gave them simple instructions. I believe we should also be doing this as a church:

> *And as you go, preach, saying, 'The kingdom of heaven is at hand.' Heal the sick, cleanse the lepers, raise the dead, cast out demons. Freely you have received, freely give.* (Mark 10:7-9)

I encourage you to try it! I haven't seen the Lord cleanse any lepers yet, but I have watched as the Holy Spirit healed the sick, raised the dead, and cast out demons. I arrived on scene after an extreme skiing accident in which a man had fallen and slid down the slope into a crevasse. He was pronounced dead, with a paramedic's testimony that he'd had no pulse for seven minutes. I began to pray, and his heart started beating again! A few months later, I met with the man so I could tell him that Jesus is the One who brought him back to life.

If you just try, God will meet you. You don't have to have super faith. Just go with what faith you have, step out and pray, and you will see miracles happen. *Freely you have received, freely give.*

CHAPTER 6

WHAT ARE DEMONS?

For some it is quite hard to imagine, and especially to believe, that there are evil spirits you cannot see, which go into people and affect their behavior. It is really a stretch for the mind, and many Christians think it just couldn't happen. After seeing people manifest evil spirits, I had to process those experiences and come to some conclusion about what was happening. The Bible is the place to turn to for answers; there we learn:

- Demons are evil and Jesus has the power to cast them out
- Jesus can give us the authority to do so as well
- The disciples were given instructions, and had the God-given authority to require demons to leave
- Jesus initially sent out his twelve disciples to cast out demons, and later sent out the seventy with the same instructions and authority

By studying the relevant scriptural passages, we learn that as followers of Christ we too are to follow the model of the twelve and the seventy to cast out demons.

But go rather to the lost sheep of the house of Israel. And as you go, preach, saying, 'The kingdom of heaven is at hand.' Heal the sick, cleanse the lepers, raise the dead, cast out demons. Freely you have received, freely give. (Matthew 10:6-10)

Demons have no physical body but are disembodied evil spirits with the ability to move through walls and ceilings. Once they enter a person, they can speak through their mouth and vocal cords, and many can reside in one body. During ministry sessions, they sometimes speak to me in English and often I wonder how many languages they know. They also speak in evil tongues that disgust me. They exhibit will, emotion, intellect and self-awareness; they can be afraid, become tired and need rest. They have names, like to negotiate, and can make people abnormally strong. They want to inhabit humans and don't want to wander about without bodies. They can leave a person and return later, as well as communicate with each other. They have information, and some can forecast the future. They can also go into animals. Above all, they know very well that Jesus is the Son of God and He has power over them.

Let's take a look at these traits, in Jesus' words:

"When an unclean spirit goes out of a man, he goes through dry places, seeking rest, and finds none. Then he says, 'I will return to my house from which I came.' And when he comes, he finds it empty, swept, and put in order. Then he goes and takes with him seven other spirits more wicked than himself, and they enter and dwell there; and the last state of that man is worse than the first." (Matthew 12:43-44)

In this scripture, the evil spirit could find no rest after leaving the man and traveling through dry places, which sounds like demons get to rest when they enter a person. Then, using its own will and intellect, the spirit decides to return to the house, or body, from which it came and takes others along too. Using this episode as an example, we conclude that an evil spirit can do the following:

- Navigate through terrestrial places and return to its former abode
- Discern if the delivered person is accessible to re-inhabit
- Find other demons that are even more evil and communicate with them
- Lead others to enter a person
- Work in teams

Clearly, after deliverance an individual needs to be filled with the Holy Spirit and not left empty or he might end up worse than before the prayer ministry. This is why we ask the person that is coming for ministry if they have received Christ. If they haven't, we lead them in a prayer of salvation. At the beginning of the session we ask the Lord to fill them with the Holy Spirit. At the end, we recommend reading the Bible each day, along with worshiping the Lord and spending time in prayer. By using these simple steps, the body, or 'house', remains filled with the Holy Spirit. We teach them to verbally war against any evil spirit that comes back around. People need to learn that as Christians they have authority against demons and can bind and send them away. As long as they continue to seek the Lord and don't go back into sin patterns the demons usually do not renter.

Demons experience fear, to the point of trembling before God, as is seen in James 2:19:

You believe that there is one God. You do well. Even the demons believe— and tremble!

In Luke 8:26-32, we learn much about demons:

Then they sailed to the country of the Gadarenes, which is opposite Galilee. And when He stepped out on the land, there met Him a certain man from the city who had demons for a long time. And he wore no clothes, nor did he live in a house but in the tombs. When he saw Jesus, he cried out, fell down before Him, and with a loud voice said, "What have I to do with You, Jesus, Son of the Most High God? I beg You, do not torment me!" For it had often seized him, and he was kept under guard, bound with chains and shackles; and he broke the bonds and was driven by the demon into the wilderness. Jesus asked him, saying, "What is your name?" And he said, "Legion," because many demons had entered him. And they begged Him that He would not command them to go out into the abyss. Now a herd of many swine was feeding there on the mountain. So they begged Him that He would permit them to enter them. And He permitted them.

To summarize, demons:

- Can suffer pain (Notice how they beg Jesus not to torment them.)
- Know very well that Jesus is the Son of the Most High God and that He has the authority over them
- Can impart demonic supernatural strength to the point that in the scripture here, he broke the chains and shackles
- Have names and know their names; in this case 'Legion' was a name that represented many demons
- May negotiate and even beg for a better deal
- May enter into animals

In Acts 19:14-17, the evil spirit was able to distinguish that the sons of Sceva were not filled with the Holy Spirit, and therefore had no authority over it. It appears that the spirit was supernaturally strong, or at least supernaturally angry!

Also there were seven sons of Sceva, a Jewish chief priest, who did so. And the evil spirit answered and said, "Jesus I know, and Paul I know; but who are you?" Then the man in whom the evil spirit was leaped on them, overpowered them, and prevailed against them, so that they fled out of that house naked and wounded. This became known both to all Jews and Greeks dwelling in Ephesus; and fear fell on them all, and the name of the Lord Jesus was magnified.

What is the origin of demons? There are four main theories:

1. They are fallen angels that fell with Satan in his rebellion against God
2. They are disembodied spirits of a pre-Adamic race that is not recorded in the Bible
3. They are spirits created when the fallen sons of God bred human women, creating giants outside the plan of God; these mighty men of renown then had sexual relations with women, producing children that were not created within God's original design. When they, or their offspring, die their spirits are not eligible to enter into God's original plan for humanity, so the spirits become demons.
4. A combination of some or all of the above

Let's backtrack and look at each of the four theories, beginning with the fallen-angels-that-fell scenario. I believe this is the least likely correct theory, and Jude 6 provides some insight. First, is the New English Translation.

You also know that the angels who did not keep within their proper domain but abandoned their own place of residence, he has kept in eternal chains in utter darkness, locked up for the judgment of the great Day.

In the Tree of Life Version, we can see that the angels that deserted their proper place are shackled.

And the angels—who did not keep their own position of authority but deserted their proper place—He has kept in everlasting shackles under gloomy darkness until the judgment of the great Day.

2 Peter 2:4 (NET) reveals that God severely punished the angels who sinned.

For if God did not spare the angels who sinned, but threw them into hell and locked them up in chains in utter darkness, to be kept until the judgment...

Based on the above scriptures, I believe that the fallen angels are kept chained in darkness, so therefore they are not demons.

Additionally, during ministry prayer sessions, demons often try to negotiate so they can stay in the person and are quite afraid that they will have to leave their human host. They don't present as fallen angelic beings that the Lord has created. I have done ministry with prayer ministers who can see in the Spirit, and what they describe is not angel-like. Sometimes people have a snake demon, and when it manifests, it causes the person to flick out their tongue and move back and forth like a snake would when a snake charmer is playing his flute. To me, this doesn't seem like the way a fallen angel would behave. Rather, it looks like the way a snake would behave. Combined with scripture, this behavior of people manifesting demons leads me to believe demons are something other than fallen angels.

The Bible does not support the disembodied-spirits-of-a-pre-Adamic-race theory. When I first heard it, I thought, "That is ridiculous". Various scholars have promoted this hypothesis throughout history, with two notable examples being Roman Emperor Julian the Apostate (circa A. D. 331–363) and Calvinist theologian Isaac de La Peyrère (1596-1676). [1]

Next is the school of thought that demons are the spirits of the children produced though the mating of fallen sons of God and human women. The first question to consider here is, who are the sons of God? In the New Testament, the saints are called the sons of God; in the Old Testament, there are fallen sons of God" that operate outside the righteousness of God.

> *That the sons of God saw the daughters of men, that they were beautiful; and they took wives for themselves of all whom they chose.* Genesis 6:2

There were giants on the earth in those days, and also afterward, when the sons of God came into the daughters of men and they bore children to them. Those were the mighty men who were of old, men of renown.
Genesis 6:4

Let's look at Genesis 6:4 again, but in the New American Standard Bible:

The Nephilim were on the earth in those days, and also afterward, when the sons of God came into the daughters of men, and they bore children to them. Those were the mighty men who were of old, men of renown.

Job 1:6 and 2:1 also refer to the fallen sons of God:

Now there was a day when the sons of God came to present themselves before the Lord, and Satan also came among them (1:6). Again there was a day when the sons of God came to present themselves before the Lord, and Satan came also among them to present himself before the Lord (2:1).

From Job we learn that these sons of God can present themselves before the Lord and that Satan can come with them. It is obvious that these sons of God are evil because they are associating with Satan. It even reads like the sons of God got the appointment before God and Satan tagged along. Who are these sons God? The Bible does not say they are fallen angels.

These sons of God somehow co-habited with women to produce the Nephilim, the Old Testament giants. These fallen sons of God could be created beings that were cast out of heaven along with Satan. It is not clear how they were using human women to produce giants, but any theories about how such a union could occur is speculative; there is no scriptural documentation regarding how these spirits could re-produce with human women. The point is, they were coming into human women and reproducing. Because the Nephilim were created outside of Gods plan, He didn't know them before they were born, and they were unable to enter into salvation and become filled with the Holy Spirit. Therefore, when they died their spirits could not enter heaven and they live in earthly realms as the spirits we know as demons.

The Sethite Theory:

In his article, *Mischievous Angels or Sethites?* Dr. Chuck Missler explains the origin of the Sethite theory:

The strange events recorded in Genesis six were understood by the ancient rabbinical sources, as well as the Septuagint translators, as referring to fallen angels who procreated weird hybrid offspring with human women known as the Nephilim. So, it was also understood by the early church fathers. These bizarre events are also echoed in the legends and myths of every ancient culture upon the earth: the ancient Greeks, the Egyptians, the Hindus, the South Sea Islanders, the American Indians, and virtually all the others.

However, many students of the Bible have been taught that this passage in Genesis 6 actually refers to failure to keep the "faithful" lines of Seth separate from the "worldly" line of Cain. The idea has been advanced that after Cain killed Abel, the line of Seth remained separate and faithful, but the line of Cain turned ungodly and rebellious. The "sons of God" are deemed to refer to leadership in the line of Seth; the "daughters of men" are deemed restricted to the line of Cain. The resulting marriages ostensibly blurred in inferred separation between them. (Why the resulting offspring are called the "Nephilim" remains without any clear explanation.)

Since Jesus prophesied, "As the days of Noah were, so shall the coming of the Son of Man be," it becomes essential to understand what these days included.
It was in the 5th Century A. D. that the "angel" interpretation of

Genesis six was increasingly viewed as an embarrassment when attacked by critics. (Furthermore, the worship of angels had begun within the church. Also, celibacy had also become an institution of the church. The "angel" view of Genesis six was feared as impacting these views.)

Celsus and Julian the Apostate used the traditional "angel" belief to attack Christianity.

Julius Africanus resorted to the Sethite interpretation as a more comfortable ground. Cyril of Alexandria also repudiated the orthodox "angel" position with the "line of Seth" interpretation. Augustine also embraced the Sethite theory and thus it prevailed into the Middle Ages. It is still widely taught today among many churches who find the literal "angel" view a bit disturbing. There are many outstanding Bible teachers who still defend this view. [2]

Both Catholic and Protestant theology was influenced by Rome, and it appears that fallen angels breeding human women did not fit well into their understanding. Developing alternative theology seemed to be a good option. George H. Pember, in his classic work written in the late 1800's, *Earth's Earliest Ages*, came to the same conclusion:

These words are often explained to signify nothing more than the intermarriage of the descendants of Cain and Seth: but a careful examination of the passage will elicit a far deeper meaning.

When men, we are told, began to multiply on the face of the earth, and daughters were born unto them, the sons of God saw the daughters of men. Now by "men" in each case the whole human race is evidently signified, the descendants of Cain and Seth alike. Hence the "sons of God" are plainly distinguished from the generation of Adam.

Again, the expression "sons of God" (Elohim) occurs four times
in other parts of the Old Testament and is in each of these
cases indisputably used of angelic beings. [3]

It should be noted that in the rabbinical literature of today, and the
early Church Fathers concluded that 'sons of God' referred to some
category of angel or created beings and not righteous men. How could
godly men marrying ungodly women produce giants? We must accept
that there were literal giants on the earth. Og, the king of Bashon,
slept on an iron bed six feet wide and fifteen feet long. [4] Let's face the
fact that these were not just large men that were created by humans
marrying and producing offspring. I agree with the "angel" position,
and I am convinced that this is critical to understanding the Bible and
spiritual warfare.

The origin of demons as a combination of some or all of the above
theories is the least likely scenario of all. Scripture does not provide us
with sufficient information to decide which of these theories, is
correct. The fact is that we don't know the origins of the demons, but
we do know that they are engaged in tormenting humans.

CHAPTER 7
DEMONS AND THE HEAVENLY PLACES

Do demons live in the heavenly places?

I believe that demons are terrestrial and stay near the earth. They seem to want to dwell inside of people, so it makes sense to think that they'd stay where the people are.

On one occasion, Anne and I waited in a jet on the runway in Lusaka, Zambia. Passengers were finished boarding, but the door of the jet was still open when I smelled the odor of sulfur. Anne, who can see in the Spirit, said, "Did you see that demon go down the aisle?" I answered that while I didn't see it, I did smell it. The sense of smell is one form of discerning of spirits. I thought it interesting that an evil spirit had decided to move from Zambia to London by aircraft!

> *Put on the whole armor of God, that you may be able to stand against the schemes of the devil. For we do not wrestle against flesh and blood, but against the rulers, against the authorities, against the cosmic powers over this present darkness, against the spiritual forces of evil in the heavenly places. Therefore, take up the whole armor of God, that you may be able to withstand in the evil day, and having done all, to stand firm.* (Ephesians 6:11-13 ESV)

This scripture is not about demons. Rulers, authorities, cosmic powers, and spiritual forces of evil are different than demons; they reside in the heavenly places, or unseen dimensions. While Jesus commonly cast demons out and taught His followers to do the same, I can find no example in the Bible of Him directly teaching us to confront evil in heavenly places. Unless you have very specific revelation from God, I strongly recommend not praying directly against them because such actions could set you apart as a target for some high-level evil. I believe that territorial spirits have a right to be where they are. If you want to ask the Lord to remove them, that would be safe; but to pray directly against them would be asking for trouble and would not conform to a biblical model. If the Lord decided to remove them, then of course He can, and if enough prayers go up, then in His timing He may do just that. He may even prompt you to ask Him to do it. I once ministered to someone who had been praying against spirits in heavenly places, and the results of my prayer were not as healing as I would have hoped. Evil had a serious grip on his mind and it was very sad to see what the enemy had done to his life, mind, and family.

John Paul Jackson wrote a good book, *Needless Casualties of War*, which gives an in-depth teaching about praying directly against evil in high places.

https://www.amazon.com/dp/158483000X

A lying spirit sent from Heaven

There is a biblical example in 1 Kings 22:18-19 of a spirit that was among the host of heaven, which became a lying spirit that God sent from Heaven to Earth. I find it interesting that such a spirit could become a lying spirit that spoke through the mouths of about four hundred prophets.

> *Then Micaiah said, "Therefore hear the word of the Lord: I saw the Lord sitting on His throne, and all the host of heaven standing by, on His right hand and on His left. And the Lord said, 'Who will persuade*

Ahab to go up, that he may fall at Ramoth Gilead?' So one spoke in this manner, and another spoke in that manner. Then a spirit came forward and stood before the Lord, and said, 'I will persuade him.' The Lord said to him, 'In what way?' So he said, 'I will go out and be a lying spirit in the mouth of all his prophets.' And the Lord said, 'You shall persuade him, and also prevail. Go out and do so.

Though we do know that demons are lying spirits, this particular spirit was different than a demon; it is sent from heaven to accomplish a specific assignment from the Lord.

Do demons die?

Demons don't die, so when their human host dies, they leave the body. Sometimes they may have a right to move on to daughters or sons of the deceased; there are many stories of this happening. Other times, they find someone else to inhabit and control. I can imagine that there is a type of hierarchy among evil beings, with the fallen sons of God and Satan at the top and the little demons that I coughed out during my first self-deliverance at the bottom. It could be that if demons do not attack humans, they may get punished from evil spirits higher up the ladder. We do know from scripture that they can be tormented because Legion specifically asked Jesus not to torment them.

Revelation 9:

Verses 1-6 speak of the fifth trumpet and locusts from the bottomless pit:

Then the fifth angel sounded: And I saw a star fallen from heaven to the earth. To him was given the key to the bottomless pit. And he opened the bottomless pit, and smoke arose out of the pit like the smoke of a great furnace. So the sun and the air were darkened because of the smoke of the pit. Then out of the smoke locusts came upon the earth. And to them was given power, as the scorpions of the earth have power. They were commanded not to harm the grass of the earth, or any green thing, or any tree, but only those men who do not have the seal of God on their foreheads. And they were not given authority to kill them, but to torment them for five months. Their torment was like the torment of a scorpion when it strikes a man. In those days men will seek death and will not find it; they will desire to die, and death will flee from them. The shape of the locusts was like horses prepared for battle. On their heads were crowns of something like gold, and their faces were like the faces of men. They had hair like women's hair, and their teeth were like lions' teeth. And they had breastplates like breastplates of iron, and the sound of their wings was like the sound of chariots with many horses running into battle. They had tails like scorpions, and there were stings in their tails. Their power was to hurt men five months. And they had as king over them the angel of the bottomless pit, whose name in Hebrew is Abaddon, but in Greek he has the name Apollyon.

Continuing on in Revelation 9:7-21, we see that the locusts with faces like men that have come out of the bottomless pit have Abaddon as a king over them. They are neither allowed to kill the people but may only torment them with stings, nor harm the grass of the earth, any green thing or tree; and may only harm those people who do not have the seal of God on their foreheads.

Although these are not demons, they do come out of the pit to torment people; and wherever demons come from, they also come to hurt people, though in other ways. The locusts are under the authority of a king; they are not just flying around randomly stinging and they are not allowed to kill. Clearly, they must follow the rules set forth by the Lord. This could also be the case with demons. When a prayer minister leads a person into a prayer of correct repentance, the legal right for the demon to be in there is broken; when the person tells it to go, it does. Before repentance, they could tell it to leave and it might not because of its legal right to remain. The demons seem to be under a legal set of rules, and when the right for them to be occupying or attached has been broken, they have to go, and they know it.

Demons are ceaseless in their attack on the human race and there are many of them. To put it in context, the demon in the Gadarene demoniac said his name was Legion, and a Roman legion in those times was composed of about six thousand men. That leads me to believe that there could have been thousands in the man Jesus healed. There seem to be enough demons to occupy the human race. Even though the human population keeps increasing on the planet, there is no shortage of demons to torment people.

The Bible includes many references to evil spirits, in both the Old and New Testaments:

- Familiar spirits: Leviticus 20:27
- Spirit of ill will: Judges 9:23
- Jealousy: Numbers 5:14, 30
- Ill will: Judges 9:23
- Distressing spirit: 1 Samuel 16:14-23, 18:10, 19:9
- Lying spirit: I Kings 22:22; 2 Chronicles 18:20-22
- Perverse spirit: Isaiah 19:14
- Spirit of deep sleep: Isaiah 29. 10
- Spirit of heaviness: Isaiah 61:3
- Spirit of harlotry: Hosea 4:12, 5:5
- Unclean spirit: Zechariah 13:2
- Mute spirit: Mark 9:17
- Deaf and dumb spirit: Mark 9:25
- Spirit of infirmity: Luke13:11
- Spirit of divination: Acts 16:16
- Spirit of bondage: Romans 8:15
- Spirit of stupor: Romans 11:8
- Spirit of the world: 1 Corinthians 2:12
- Spirit of fear: 1 Timothy 1:7
- Deceiving spirits: 1 Timothy 4:1
- Spirit of the antichrist: 1 John 4:3
- Spirit of error: 1 John 4:6
- Foul spirit: Revelation 18:2

Just to be clear, in the above list there is not one spirit with righteous intent; whether they are various evil spirits or specifically demons, all are intent on nothing less than destruction toward mankind.

> *Be sober, be vigilant; because your adversary the devil walks about like a roaring lion, seeking whom he may devour. Resist him, steadfast in the faith, knowing that the same sufferings are experienced by your brother-hood in the world.* 1 Peter 5:8-9

CHAPTER 8

DO DEMONS AFFLICT
CHRISTIANS?

Personal experience is never a good way to establish biblical doctrine, but when something spiritual is happening right before your eyes, it needs to be biblically explained.

For fifteen years of my Christian life I had an incorrect doctoral belief that Christians could not have demons in them. I believed that when you are saved, you are set completely free from the powers of darkness; you move from the kingdom of darkness into the kingdom of light. When you are filled with light then there can be no room for darkness, for of course there cannot be both the Holy Spirit and an evil spirit living within the same vessel.

> *Therefore take heed that the light which is in you is not darkness. If then your whole body is full of light, having no part dark, the whole body will be full of light, as when the bright shining of a lamp gives you light.* (Luke 11:35-36)

> *Then Jesus spoke to them again, saying, "I am the light of the world. He who follows Me shall not walk in darkness, but have the light of life."* (John 8:12)

I believed that demons could come around me and affect my thinking, but they could not be inside of me. While praying for people in Zambia, hundreds were manifesting demons; I believed that I was immune to those I cast out because I was filled with the light of the Holy Spirit. I didn't understand that I could have been born with some demons and that they were affecting my health and my thinking.

After the Nakonde out-door meeting, the Lord started leading me to learn more about the subject of evil affecting Christians. Then I found out that a close Christian friend had manifested a demon in another friend's kitchen during prayer. In my mind, it simply came down to the fact that either my close friend was not saved, or my doctrine was wrong. I realized that my friend was definitely saved; she had attended church with me for years, and was sold out for Jesus. In fact, she was as saved as I was, so her not being a Christian was not a valid option to explain her manifestation. The only other option was that my doctrinal beliefs were wrong. I would have to study the Bible and discuss the situation with trusted Christian teachers to find where my misunderstanding lay.

Some people quote 2 Corinthians 5:17 to support the idea that Christians cannot have a demon:

Therefore, if anyone is in Christ, he is a new creation; old things have passed away; behold, all things have become new.

Of course, the believer is a new creation in Christ. His or her spirit has been regenerated and has been born again; but to use this scripture to conclude that all demons have left and all curses are broken is a stretch, to say the least. Demons occupy both the soul and the body, and this scripture is speaking about the spirit. If it were about the flesh, then all sickness would also pass away when one becomes a new creation, and clearly people who are saved can still get sick.

Others quote John 8:36 for the same reason:

Therefore if the Son makes you free, you shall be free indeed.

True, if the Son sets you free, then you will really be free, which is exactly what is happening during a deliverance prayer session as they confess their sins and demons are cast out. This is when they are indeed free of that evil spirit. Of course, the Lord can also sovereignly deliver you from demons, even when you don't ask, and I believe some of them may leave when you accept Christ and are baptized in the Spirit. In my personal experience, though, many stayed even after I was baptized in the Spirit, and I've observed the same thing in others during ministry sessions.

Yes, Jesus's blood is sufficient to cleanse us from all sin and evil. When we come to Him, confessing our sins with heartfelt repentance, He surely will deliver us and break our generational curses. While some deliverance just happens along with salvation, we also must walk out our sanctification. It is not automatic; we must come to Him and humbly ask for help. In my life, I needed prayer ministers with wisdom and authority who knew how to pray according to the leading of the Holy Spirit and who had enough authority that when they told the evil spirits to go, they obeyed.

Another scripture I hear people quote is 2 Corinthians 3: 14-18, saying out of context, "Where the Spirit of the Lord is, there is liberty. " But in context, you can see that it is speaking about the veil that blocks understanding in the reading of the Old Testament, which is taken away in Christ. When the veil is removed, then there is liberty and we can be transformed from glory to glory. It is a process, not an instant event that accomplishes total deliverance.

> *But their minds were blinded. For until this day the same veil remains unlifted in the reading of the Old Testament, because the veil is taken away in Christ. But even to this day, when Moses is read, a veil lies on their heart. Nevertheless when one turns to the Lord, the veil is taken away. Now the Lord is the Spirit; and where the Spirit of the Lord is, there is liberty. But we all, with unveiled face, beholding as in a mirror the glory of the Lord, are being transformed into the same image from glory to glory, just as by the Spirit of the Lord.*

Randy Clark sums it up well in *The Biblical Guidebook to Deliverance*:[1]

> I believe all things demonic were dealt with on the Cross, including generational curses, but we must appropriate the benefits of the finished work of Christ for ourselves in order to receive their benefit.

https://www.amazon.com/dp/B00U58QKJM

This side of the cross:

One theory that I run across quite often is that Jesus was both doing deliverance and teaching His disciples to do deliverance because they were living in the time before Jesus died on the cross; but now that we are on this side of His resurrection and the power of the Holy Spirit has been released, deliverance is no longer necessary. They argue that when a person is filled with the Holy Spirit, no evil spirit can live within a person at the same time as the Holy Spirit. They claim, "It was all finished on the cross. "

There seem to be two camps:

1. When you are saved, all the demons leave and all the generational rights are broken.
2. When you are saved, all the demons leave and the generational rights remain.

In Matthew 10:7, Jesus taught:

And as you go, preach, saying, "The kingdom of heaven is at hand. Heal the sick, cleanse the lepers, raise the dead, cast out demons."

There's a problem here for both schools of thought because if all demons were required to leave a Christian immediately after salvation and being filled with the Spirit, why didn't Jesus build in an exclusion clause or add further instruction regarding how we are to minister now? In reality, all people need to do to find out if demons can occupy Christians this side of the cross is to observe a deliverance prayer session and watch what the Lord does. It will soon become obvious when a Christian manifests a demon and is set free, that we do indeed need deliverance.

CHAPTER 9
BODY, SOUL AND SPIRIT

et's talk about how the light of the Holy Spirit can indwell someone at the same time they are suffering in the darkness of the demons, beginning with 1 Thessalonians 5:23:

Now may the God of peace Himself sanctify you completely; and may your whole spirit, soul, and body be preserved blameless at the coming of our Lord Jesus Christ.

Clearly, we are three-part beings who have a body, soul and spirit. When we are saved, the Holy Spirit comes into us and regenerates[1] our spirit; we are redeemed;[2] we become new creatures in Christ, and are then seated in the heavens.[3] Our regenerated spirit, which is owned by Christ and sealed by the Holy Spirit,[4] cannot be entered or possessed by demonic spirits.

The Body:

Demons operate in the body; the woman in Luke 18:11 had a spirit of infirmity in her body, which caused her to be bent over.

And behold, there was a woman who had a spirit of infirmity eighteen years, and was bent over and could in no way raise herself up. But when Jesus saw her, He called her to Him and said to her, "Woman, you are loosed from your infirmity." And He laid His hands on her, and immediately she was made straight, and glorified God.

A few years ago, I had a spirit of infirmity that caused an intense pain in my right side, just below the rib cage. It started mildly the day before Albie Pearson came to speak at our church while I was on a three-hour bike ride, and it kept getting more and more painful. The next day I went to hear Albie preach. During the sermon and after the service the pain intensified, so much so that I was ready to drive to the Emergency Room. I suspected it was a demon harassing me and wanted Albie to pray for me, but people kept talking to him and then a young man began to prophesy. In tremendous pain and waiting for prayer, the prophesy went on and on! My friend Tom Griner was there, and I told him about the pain. He asked me if there was anyone I needed to forgive. The only one I could think of was my ex-wife, whom I had forgiven her many times; but the pain was so bad I repented once more for un-forgiveness. After Tom prayed, I got in the car to drive to the hospital. As I got to a stop sign, my side hurt so badly that I was afraid of passing out. Breathing heavily and at the limit of my pain tolerance, I thought, "If I turn right and get to the hospital, then I can get some morphine." Medical help was fifteen miles away, and I was only a couple minutes from my house where I could get into bed to see if things improved. I turned left.

Curled in a fetal position in bed, sweating and breathing heavily, I wondered if I could take this any longer. After twenty minutes, the pain was subsiding, and over the next twenty-four hours it resolved completely. The next day I made a doctor's appointment to see if there was a physical problem behind the pain. They performed a CAT scan and a bunch of tests that cost five thousand dollars. After a few days, the doctor called me into the office to give the results of the tests and said that I was fine. I answered, "It must have been the demon." She looked at me and said jokingly, "It must have been." A couple of years later I was speaking after church to a young woman that told me she had a pain in her right side, and that she was going to Reno for tests. I said that I'd experienced that same problem before and it was caused by a demon, and then told her that if the doctors couldn't find anything, my wife and I would be willing to pray for her. After seeing doctors and having and all the diagnostic tests, the doctors could not find anything wrong with her and were planning exploratory surgery. She chose prayer.

The first time she came for prayer she didn't get healed, and the next time we spoke, she said the pain had moved to the left side. I then knew that it was a demon because demons can move around in the body. We set up another prayer session, and when I walked into the prayer room, she was laying on the floor receiving prayer from our group of Thursday afternoon intercessors. I asked her how she was feeling, and she answered that she had been fine all day until I walked into the room, but now she was now in pain. I thought to myself, "You foul spirit!" Anne, Anna Glover, and I ministered to her, cast out several spirits, and she was healed.

The soul:

The soul consists of the mind, will and emotions,[5] and demonic spirits can operate in each of these areas; often, demons cause chemical imbalances that lead to mental illness. Doctors are able to determine through brain scans the part of the mind that is being stimulated and can medicate the brain. In changing the chemical balance, they cause improvement in a person's behavior or mental health. That's only a partial fix, because while the drugs may control or suppress an issue, they cannot heal it completely. Only Jesus can bring the necessary deliverance and administer true healing for mental illnesses that are caused by demonization.

The spirit:

The New Testament is clear: we are triune beings. As I researched what the spirit of man is, I could feel my spirit rise up; it literally woke up or came more forward. I could feel a spiritual alertness in the front of my mind behind my forehead, and I felt like my spirit came 'over' or took leadership of my soul. This is where the spirit belongs, on top, in leadership with the soul and body underneath or following.

The spirit—what a wonderful elusive part of us. I like what Barbara Parker wrote in *Exploring Heavenly Places, Volume One*:

> We understand the body because we can see and touch it; and we have a fair comprehension of the soul because it is generally understood to have to do with our mind, will and emotion. But, what of the spirit? It is so much more esoteric, and every '-ism that exists seem to offer a different slant on it. Perhaps some of the confusion is because the triune being of man exists in a multidimensional universe of which he has little or no comprehension. Many may assume that if something is outside the realms of time and space it doesn't really exist but is simply make-believe or science fiction.[6]

https://www.amazon.com/dp/B00OFDFU58

Yes, I agree, it is quite esoteric. In Hebrew, the word for spirit is *ruach* and in Greek it is *pneuma*, which denotes blowing or breathing. Like our breath blowing you cannot see it, yet without our spirit we are no longer alive.

Some teach that the soul and the spirit are the same thing and that they are used interchangeably in the Bible. I don't agree with that teaching. Although they are tied closely, they are definitely different individual parts of our being. We can learn that there is a distinct difference in Hebrews 4:12:

> *For the word of God is living and powerful, and sharper than any two-edged sword, piercing even to the division of soul and spirit, and of joints and marrow, and is a discerner of the thoughts and intents of the heart.*

We know that God is the creator of man's spirit from Zechariah 12:1:

The burden of the word of the Lord against Israel. Thus says the Lord,
who stretches out the heavens, lays the foundation of the earth, and
forms the spirit of man within him:

Our spirit is what allows us to communicate with God. We receive revelation from the Spirit of God communicating with our spirit. When the Holy Spirit comes into a person, their spirit is regenerated, which allows it to communicate more clearly with the Holy Spirit. Job 32:8 says:

But there is a spirit in man, And the breath of the Almighty gives him
understanding.

I find it interesting that our spirit and soul are so closely tied together. Our soul is associated with physical life, and death occurs when it departs. The same is true of the spirit: if our spirit leaves, we are no longer living:

For as the body without the spirit is dead, so faith without works is
dead also. (James 2:26)
And so it was, as her soul was departing (for she died), that she called
his name Ben-Oni; but his father called him Benjamin. (Genesis 35:18)

Our soul can enter the Kingdom of Heaven and so can our spirit. They are tied together, but are separate facets of our being:

And I saw thrones, and they sat on them, and judgment was committed
to them. Then I saw the souls of those who had been beheaded for their
witness to Jesus and for the word of God, who had not worshiped the
beast or his image, and had not received his mark on their foreheads or
on their hands. And they lived and reigned with Christ for a thousand
years. (Revelation 20:4)

Our spirit, led by the Holy Spirit, should lead our soul and body. Proverbs 22:5 teaches:

> *Thorns and snares are in the way of the perverse; He who guards his soul will be far from them.*

In other words, he that lets his spirit lead his soul will be far from thorns and snares. With our spirit following the Holy Spirit we can walk in the fruit of the Spirit and, in turn, be blessed:

> *By humility and the fear of the Lord Are riches and honor and life. Thorns and snares are in the way of the perverse; He who guards his soul will be far from them.* (Proverbs 22:4-5)

Can a Christian be possessed by a demon?

The word 'possessed' does not appear anywhere in the New Testament in reference to demons, though some Bible translations incorrectly translates the Greek word *daimonizomai* as possessed. This has caused much confusion in the church.

Many years ago, the word 'possessed' was used differently than it is today. When one rented a house and moved into it, they were said to have possessed the house, in the same way that we use the word 'occupy'. That is why they translated *daimonizomai* as possessed. We now use that to insinuate ownership. It really helps me when reading the Bible and it says, "demon-possessed", to realize that translation really means 'demon-occupied'.

Using 'possessed' would be the equivalent of saying that a Christian is owned by demons or by the devil, which is incorrect. Christians have been bought and paid for by Jesus' blood that was shed on the cross; we belong to God.

> *For you were bought at a price; therefore glorify God in your body and in your spirit, which are God's.* (1 Corinthians 6:20)

For he who is called in the Lord while a slave is the Lord's freedman. Likewise he who is called while free is Christ's slave. You were bought at a price; do not become slaves of men. (1 Corinthians 7:22-23)

Let your conduct be without covetousness; be content with such things as you have. For He Himself has said, "I will never leave you nor forsake you." (Hebrews 13:5)

Even though evil is out to separate us from the love of God it will never happen, for we are more that conquerors through Him.

Yet in all these things we are more than conquerors through Him who loved us. For I am persuaded that neither death nor life, nor angels nor principalities nor powers, nor things present nor things to come, nor height nor depth, nor any other created thing, shall be able to separate us from the love of God which is in Christ Jesus our Lord. (Romans 8:37-39)

We have been redeemed. The literal meaning of redeemed is 'brought back'. At the fall, mankind transferred his allegiance from God to Satan and his evil powers. Through the sacrifice of Jesus on the cross, God redeemed those who would believe, repent and receive His salvation. He bought us back; He 'repossessed' us, and the price that was paid for our redemption was the blood of His Son.

CHAPTER 10
DEMONIC RIGHTS

This is quite a large subject! For this reason, the topic of demonic rights to afflict us is broken down into several chapters that include just some of the behaviors or sins that open us up to demonization. It is by no means an exhaustive list of possibilities, and some are issues that have quickly come to my mind while writing, which will hopefully increase understanding of how this all happens. The focus of this chapter is generational rights.

What are generational rights?

A generational right develops when sin committed by an ancestor has created a legal right for evil to enter or affect an individual in the present day. Through time spent in ministry, it has become apparent that the majority of demons gain entry to a person through generational sins, but demonization may also be the result of personal sinful choices, which will be discussed later. Scripture is very clear that the consequences of sin are severe and travel down the generational line:

> *You shall not make for yourself a carved image—any likeness of anything that is shall not bow down to them nor serve them. For I, the*

Lord your God, am a jealous God, visiting the iniquity of the fathers upon the children to the third and fourth generations of those who hate Me, but showing mercy to thousands, to those who love Me and keep My commandments. (Exodus 20:4-6)

The Lord is long-suffering and abundant in mercy, forgiving iniquity and transgression; but He by no means clears the guilty, visiting the iniquity of the fathers on the children to the third and fourth generation. (Numbers 14:18)

...you shall not bow down to them nor serve them. For I, the Lord your God, am a jealous God, visiting the iniquity of the fathers upon the children to the third and fourth generations of those who hate Me. (Deuteronomy 5:9)

I can find no biblical evidence that says the Lord is no longer visiting the iniquity of the fathers upon the children since Christ's atoning death on the cross. Furthermore, we can see that generational curses remain in effect when ministering. Think about the vast number of ancestral sin issues we may have inherited; we each have two parents, four grandparents, eight great-grandparents, and sixteen great-great grandparents for a total of thirty ancestors in just the last four generations whose sins can provide legal rights for curses and demonic harassment. It is clear biblically that the curses may extend down for three to four generations. If the successive generations continue the sinful behaviors, the curse keeps going down the line. If they stop, the curse is finished or broken.

An interesting question to ponder is: When someone is cursed in the following generations, will they be enticed by evil to duplicate the same original sin that empowered the curse? Of course, the answer is they are likely to do so under the demonic influence that has been inherited. That sin then sets the demonic influence to continue for another three to four generations. How many generations could this continue? Through ministry, prophetic visions and words of knowledge, I have learned that the curses keep on being renewed for many more than three to four generations. Unless someone in the bloodline becomes a Christian, repents for the behavior on behalf of the generational line and himself, and then asks the Lord to remove the consequences of the generational sin, such curses can continue on for many generations. What or who besides our triune God could break the curses?

Repenting for the sins on behalf of the ancestral line is called identificational repentance, and it breaks the legal right of evil to affect you. Jeremiah 3:24-25 provides a biblical example:

> *For shame has devoured the labor of our fathers from our youth—Their*
> *flocks and their herds, Their sons and their daughters. We lie down in*
> *our shame, And our reproach covers us. For we have sinned against the*
> *Lord our God, We and our fathers, From our youth even to this day,*
> *And have not obeyed the voice of the Lord our God.*

The effect of generational iniquity doesn't come down consistently to every child in the next three to four generations. For example, if a husband rages and beats his wife but doesn't repent unto the Lord for his behavior, his behavior could set up an inherited right for spirits of rage to afflict the children of the next three to four generations. These spirits could enter even while the children are in the womb as well as when they mature. Interviewing someone seeking prayer for this problem and asking if all their siblings suffer from rage, you will often see that not all will have the problem. The condition may also skip a generation and keep on going from there.

CHAPTER 11
PERSONAL SIN

Personal sin can open us up to demonization, and the Ten Commandments is a good place to begin looking at what God teaches on this subject. Committing any of these sins could open a door to demons.

> *You shall not take the name of the Lord your God in vain, for the Lord will not hold him guiltless who takes His name in vain... Honor your father and your mother, that your days may be long upon the land which the Lord your God is giving you. You shall not murder. You shall not commit adultery. You shall not steal. You shall not bear false witness against your neighbor. You shall not covet your neighbor's house; you shall not covet your neighbor's wife, nor his male servant, nor his female servant, nor his ox, nor his donkey, nor anything that is your neighbor's.* (Exodus 20:7, 12-17)

Some might argue that we are no longer under the Law, but that doesn't remove our responsibility not to sin. We must always remember that while the Law of Moses was limited to the Old Testament, personal responsibility for moral behavior was not. Throughout the Bible, the message is very clear that God loves righteousness and hates unrighteousness. Though Christians are under grace, we are still encouraged to become conformed to the image of Christ, who was sinless.

Lack of Forgiveness:

When ministering, I always look for a lack of forgiveness because it opens one up to demonic access. In the parable of the wicked servant in Matthew 18, the Lord taught that we must forgive others as He has forgiven us or the Father will turn us over to the torturers, which are demons. Jesus was saying that we would be subject to their afflictions if we refuse to forgive. In time, due to un-forgiveness, the Father allows the demons to affect us.

In ministry, we see over and over again that there is demonization when people haven't forgiven those who have hurt them. Through forgiveness, as well as repentance for un-forgiveness, the legal rights for the demons to remain are broken and they can be cast out easily.

"But that servant went out and found one of his fellow servants who owed him a hundred denarii; and he laid hands on him and took him by the throat, saying, 'Pay me what you owe!' So his fellow servant fell down at his feet and begged him, saying, 'Have patience with me, and I will pay you all.' And he would not, but went and threw him into prison till he should pay the debt. So when his fellow servants saw what had been done, they were very grieved, and came and told their master all that had been done. Then his master, after he had called him, said to him, 'You wicked servant! I forgave you all that debt because you begged me. Should you not also have had compassion on your fellow servant, just as I had pity on you?' And his master was angry, and delivered him to the torturers until he should pay all that was due to him. "So My heavenly Father also will do to you if each of you, from his heart, does not forgive his brother his trespasses. " (Matthew 18:28-35)

It is also important to forgive yourself because self-blame and condemnation allow access for evil because they are contrary to God's truth as expressed in Romans 8:1:

There is therefore now no condemnation to those who are in Christ Jesus, who do not walk according to the flesh, but according to the Spirit.

To walk in freedom, it is also important to forgive God if there is any resentment toward Him. Some people blame God and hold Him accountable when tragic events happen in life, but we must not allow that to occur. In ministry, you can encourage those who are holding a grudge against God to accept life as it comes, believing that He is a loving Father who cares immensely for them.

Sin in Dreams:

I have a theory that I would like to share. It could be possible that we are accountable to some degree for the sin we commit in our dreams. My friend, Barbara, who is quite gifted with dream interpretation doesn't agree with me on this, but I came to this conclusion because of a personal experience.

Anne and I had been ministering at our church. During the deliverance session, I had cast a spirit of fear out of a woman. Afterward, I drove home and took a nap before attending the church elders' meeting. While asleep, I began to have a vivid dream in which a woman was standing in a circle of my friends. I knew that she had a demon and it needed to be cast out. I said to my friends, "I got it!" and told the demon to leave using *the power of my own flesh*. Because of my sin of working from my flesh in order to show off to my friends, I had sinned. The demon then came out of the woman and began to come toward me—I could see it stretching across from her to into me. I cried out in a loud voice for help saying, "Help me! Help me! It is coming into me!" My friends just watched; there was nothing they could do, and I awoke as the evil spirit came into me and sat up in bed. I was full of adrenalin and felt uneasy and had a lack of peace. I wondered if the spirit had really come into me or if I was just upset from the dream. But I got up and went to the church elders meeting, still feeling terrible, unsettled, and totally lacking peace. I realized that the demon had really entered me during the dream. The next morning, I called my friend Anna, and she cast it out. I felt it come up and out of my throat as it left and immediately felt the peace of God return to me.

What right did this spirit have to follow me home and to come into me? That sprit hated me and knew how to cause me to sin. Somehow, it scripted a dream and put it into my mind. If I had been humble and asked the Lord to remove the spirit out of the person in the dream, the spirit would have been powerless. Because in my pride, I cast the spirit out with my flesh and sinned. Because of my sin, I gave the spirit a legal right to enter me, and so it did. It didn't matter that my sin was during a dream; it still created a demonic right to enter me, and indeed it did for real! I now believe that we should fight sin in our dreams just as we do while we are awake. Many times now, I have made righteous choices in my dreams.

Before I received deliverance prayer, I would often have perverted sexual dreams and would wake up disgusted and feeling down from the dreams. I would get out of bed and say to myself, "Oh well, it was just a dream. There is nothing I can do to change my dreams. I think I will just get dressed and go to work. " I didn't understand that there were evil legal rights that were allowing these vile dreams to come into my mind. Through prayer ministry we can break the right for evil to script dreams and to download them into our minds. I don't have that type of dream anymore. I have been set free and healed of that type of dream. Prayer ministry can change your dreams. Jesus is a dream changer. I am living proof of this.

Inner Vows:

While ministering to someone, I am always watching for some kind of inner vow that may have been taken. Vows that we set up in our mind can take effect and set up evil patterns that leave us stuck in wrong thinking. Let's use the example of a woman who was used by a man to get sex, perhaps lied to by the man who pretended to care for her but really only had an agenda to use her for sexual pleasure and then leave her. This, of course, would be painful to the woman and she might think or say, "I will never let someone get that close to me again. I will always be careful not to let another man be so close to me so I cannot get hurt again. " That would be an inner vow that could affect her spiritually from then on in a variety of ways, not the least of which could be preventing godly intimacy with her future husband.

Inner vows are common when we make an unspoken but conscious decision to do or not to do something in the future. They may include promises to oneself that begin with words such as, "I'll never..." or, "From now on, I will always..." Such vows often lock us into an unrighteous cycle of thoughts or actions. Those need to be broken through prayer to enable us to move into freedom.

Tattoos:

In a culture where a person is just about as likely to have a tattoo as not, Leviticus 19:28 is worth considering:

You shall not make any cuttings in your flesh for the dead, nor tattoo any marks on you: I am the Lord.

I was walking by a tattoo studio in downtown Sacramento and decided to go in to look at the art that was on display to indicate what tattoos were offered. Predominately, there were faces of demons, nude women and other things that were generally quite evil. I could discern a lack of freedom in the place and watched while someone got a tattoo. The artist was wiping the blood from the person's arm then injecting the ink over and over. Later, I wondered why that seemed so unholy, and then realized it was a blood pact with evil. Additionally, someone who works in a tattoo store has access to your blood on a piece of gauze, which makes the customer vulnerable to its possible use in a blood ritual. Also, if the ink that is used has been dedicated to evil, that tattoo becomes the means of evil actually injected into the body.

How do people decide what they want tattooed on them? Obviously, it's individualized, but a marijuana leaf is a statement to others that marijuana is something approved of and used. Or it might be a sexual tattoo or a skull-and-crossbones tattoo, carrying clear messages of mortality and death. Could it be possible that the unclean spirits in the people are influencing what they decide to tattoo on themselves?

Could a spirit attached to *pharmakeia* be selecting the tattoo to broadcast to others with the same spirit? Can the spirit of lust choose a sexual tattoo? Could a spirit of death inspire a skull? Of course, they could.

Some Christians believe it is fine to have a tattoo because the tattoo is a Bible scripture. Others say their tattoo artist is a Christian, so it is acceptable. My question is, "Why do you want to conform to the world?"

And do not be conformed to this world, but be transformed by the renewing of your mind, that you may prove what is that good and acceptable and perfect will of God. (Romans 12:2)

Tattoos are now in style, both in the secular world and in the Church. The reason people want them is to be like the world, to be cool, to fit in, to make a statement. It's an attempt to conform to the image of others rather than to the image of Christ. One would think that an open invitation for an infestation of evil would be enough to prohibit one from considering a tattoo, but research also shows a host of reports of ink complications, infections, toxin effects, scarring, burns, chronic irritations and much more. [1] How much better to just avoid them!

When ministering to people with tattoos, I ask them what the meaning is of each one. The answers can help me create prayers that will lead them to freedom. Some tattoos might show racism, misogyny, gang affiliations, or the presence of an unloving spirit. After praying through the effects of each tattoo, I then lead them in a prayer asking the Lord to break all blood pacts and remove all consequences from getting the tattoos.

CHAPTER 12
OCCULT PRACTICES

'Occult' means 'hidden'; and behind the practices of psychic reading, palm reading, and tarot cards are hidden demonic powers. People don't realize this. Thus, they are drawn to such practices for entertainment or to gather information that is seemingly unavailable elsewhere. The fact that it is spiritual attracts people because the supernatural is mysterious and tempting to explore. But again, they do not realize the evil to which they are being subjected. The psychics may believe they are using neutral spiritual power, totally unaware that they are receiving demonic information, or they may know exactly what they are doing.

In Acts 16:16-18, the slave girl with a python spirit of divination was able to tell the future, and revealed things about people through demonic knowledge:

> *Now it happened, as we went to prayer, that a certain slave girl*
> *possessed with a spirit of divination [of python, a seeress of Delphi] met*
> *us, who brought her masters much profit by fortune-telling. This girl*
> *followed Paul and us, and cried out, saying, "These men are the servants*
> *of the Most High God, who proclaim to us the way of salvation."And*
> *this she did for many days. But Paul, greatly annoyed, turned and said*

to the spirit, "I command you in the name of Jesus Christ to come out of her." And he came out that very hour.

This power is still in operation today, and people moving in the occult can also access supernatural information from evil spirits.

Some background on the Python is worth noting. Located on the mainland of Greece, the *omphalos* of Delphi (the stone the Greeks believed marked the center of the earth) can still be found among the ruins of Apollo's Delphic temple. So important was Apollo's oracle at Delphi that wherever Hellenism existed, its citizens and kings, including some from as far away as Spain, ordered their lives and wars by its sacred communications. It was here that the Olympian gods spoke to mortal men through the use of a priesthood, who interpreted the trance-induced utterances of the Pythoness of Pythia. She was a middle-aged woman who sat on a copper-and-gold tripod, or much earlier, on the "rock of the sibyls" (medium), and crouched over a fire while inhaling the smoke of burning laurel leaves, barley, marijuana, and oil, until a sufficient intoxication for her prophecies had been produced. Delphic 'women of python' prophesied in this way for nearly a thousand years and were an important part of Hellenistic society.

Delphi with its surrounding area, in which the famous oracle ordained and approved the worship of Asclepius, was earlier known by the name Pytho, a chief city of Phocis. In Greek mythology, Python - the namesake of the city of Pytho - was the great serpent who dwelt in the mountains of Parnassus.... In Acts 16:16, the demonic woman who troubled Paul was possessed with a spirit of divination. In Greek this means a spirit of python (seeress of Delphi, a pythoness) ...[and] reflects... the accepted Jewish belief... that the worship of Asclepius [Appllo's son] and other such idolatries were, as Paul would later articulate in 1 Corinthians 10:20 the worship of demons. [1]

In Acts 19:19 the people had recognized God's holy power and turned away from the evil power they had been aligned with, destroying some very expensive books in an act of repentance:

Also, many of those who had practiced magic brought their books together and burned them in the sight of all. And they counted up the value of them, and it totaled fifty thousand pieces of silver.

Other scriptures also speak of dangers associated with occult practices:

Also, he caused his sons to pass through the fire in the Valley of the Son of Hinnom; he practiced soothsaying, used witchcraft and sorcery, and consulted mediums and spiritists. He did much evil in the sight of the Lord, to provoke Him to anger. (2 Chronicles 33:6)

When you come into the land which the Lord your God is giving you, you shall not learn to follow the abominations of those nations. There shall not be found among you anyone who makes his son or his daughter pass through the fire, or one who practices witchcraft, or a soothsayer, or one who interprets omens, or a sorcerer, or one who conjures spells, or a medium, or a spiritist, or one who calls up the dead. For all who do these things are an abomination to the Lord, and because of these abominations the Lord your God drives them out from before you. (Deuteronomy 18:9-12)

Cursed Objects and Cursed Buildings:

Evil can attach to objects and buildings, so we must be certain that we only enter places or own objects that are spiritually clean.

Yes, there are real haunted houses! But ghosts are not the problem —demons are. If someone makes an object, prays over it or uses it in an evil religious ceremony, evil can attach to it. Then, if that object is brought into a house, it can affect the atmosphere. Second-hand jewelry is another place to be careful; it should always be discerned before wearing because if evil is attached, it can affect the person who wears it.

One common thing people do when traveling is to buy scary-looking wooden masks that are used in ceremonies; they are always on sale in African countries. I strenuously recommend avoiding them. I went to a market in Lusaka, Zambia where idols that had been worshiped in villages for hundreds of years were being sold. The idol salesman even told me, "They are very old and very powerful. " Unknowing people buy and bring them home and end up changing the spiritual atmosphere of their home. Sometimes the wood or stone carvers pray over an object inviting the evil to attach to them; this also happens with occult manufacturers of jewelry who hope to 'bless' the wearer with the presence of their favorite spirit.

Albie Pearson told me about a pastor who had brought an object back from Africa and put it on his desk. While Albie was meeting with him, they heard a lot of noise coming from the pastor's office. When they checked to see what had happened, they saw that books had been thrown off the shelves and everything had flown around the room. Once they realized the object from Africa was the problem, they removed it and prayed over the office, after which there was no more trouble.

Entering Temples:

While traveling in southern China, I was hiking up a mountain near Shantou that had some beautiful granite boulders covering it. I came to a large Buddhist temple. Inside I could see many monks chanting and could discern an intense evil emanating out of the temple. People have reported picking up demons when they visited pagan temples, so I do not recommend visiting them while traveling. If you remove your shoes before entering, you honor their god and give the associated demons a right to come against you. Additionally, if there is already a generational right of which you were unaware, perhaps even hundreds or thousands of years back, the demonic could be activated and you could go home with a lot more than a few colorful pictures.

Games:

Many popular games, whether board or video games, are infested with demonic influence and should be shunned. Ouija Boards are one of the worst offenders and are actually sometimes called spirit or talking boards. [2] Any use of such games is a wide-open invitation to demons, and past use should be dealt with in prayer.

Idolatry and False Religions:

Exodus 20:3-4 makes it very clear that God is a jealous God, and that having any other gods besides Him is a sin.

You shall have no other gods before Me. You shall not make for yourself a carved image—any likeness of anything that is in heaven above, or that is in the earth beneath, or that is in the water under the earth; you shall not bow down to them nor serve them. For I, the Lord your God, am a jealous God, visiting the iniquity of the fathers upon the children to the third and fourth generations of those who hate Me, but showing mercy to thousands, to those who love Me and keep My commandments.

There is one true God, Adonai, the God of the Hebrews. All other gods are false gods. There is only one way to the Father and that is through the Son, Jesus Christ.

Jesus said to him, "I am the way, the truth, and the life. No one comes to the Father except through Me." (John 14:6)

All attempts to get to heaven or obtain enlightenment and eternal life that are not through Jesus Christ are false paths, created by evil to deceive people and lead them away from the truth. Such false religious pursuits open us up to demonization.

CHAPTER 13
THE UNGODLY POWER OF WORDS

The Tongue

When we speak, we affect the spiritual realm. There is power in our words, which are not just vibrations of sound moving through the air. Words are so much more, and they have definite spiritual effects. For example, if we bind something on earth it is bound in heaven, and when we loose things on earth they are loosed in heaven. [1] We do that through our spoken words. When we tell a demon to leave someone, it is the words that have the God-given authority to drive out the spirit, and the demons hear and obey. With our words we pray and the Lord hears and responds; with our words we can both bless the Lord and curse men, so we must watch what we say or we can sin with our mouths, opening up rights for evil spirits to afflict us as well as others. Such things as gossip, lying and unjust criticism open doors for evil, and as James illustrated so well, this should not be the case:

Even so the tongue is a little member and boasts great things. See how great a forest a little fire kindles! And the tongue is a fire, a world of iniquity. The tongue is so set among our members that it defiles the whole body, and sets on fire the course of nature; and it is set on fire by hell. For every kind of beast and bird, of reptile and creature of the sea, is tamed and has been tamed by mankind. But no man can tame the tongue. It is an unruly evil, full of deadly poison. With it we bless our God and Father, and with it we curse men, who have been made in the similitude of God. Out of the same mouth proceed blessing and cursing. My brethren, these things ought not to be so. (James 3:5-10)

Self-Cursing:

A self-curse can be spoken out loud or can be just a thought in the mind. Have you ever heard someone say, "I would be better off dead," or, "I am sick and tired". These are sayings we pick up in life and utter thoughtlessly. Jesus warned us about speaking idle or empty words,[2] and any time we think or say something negative over ourselves, it can become a curse. For example, we may be struggling in a class at school and say," I will never pass this class!" These are actually self-curses. I am glad that usually they don't stick, but sometimes they do, and need to be broken in prayer.

Secret Societies:

Secret societies often require verbal commitments, or vows, that tie a person to evil. At the lower levels of Freemasonry, for example, members are told that they can be Christians and Masons at the same time without compromise. Then they take their vows and go through the ceremonies to move up to higher and higher levels, quite uneducated about what the organization represents. They don't realize that at the higher levels members actually end up worshiping Satan. If anyone has Freemasonry in the bloodline or has joined the Masons, they are tied to extremely powerful evil entities that should be broken through prayer. Aslan's Place has a good written prayer to dismantle the effects of Freemasonry. [3]

CHAPTER 14
ADDICTIONS

Pornography

Jesus taught about adultery in Matthew 5:28:

> *But I say to you that whoever looks at a woman to lust for her has already committed adultery with her in his heart.*

For you to even think lustful thoughts about a woman or man is to commit adultery in your heart. This scripture applies to married men, but the principle also applies to wives who entertain lustful thoughts toward other men. You can see the danger of pornography here. If one is unmarried, it is still sin but is called fornication even though it occurs in one's heart. Jesus' words here are very helpful because we learn that it is not just the physical act that is sin, but also the thought itself. Even though pornography is just pictures displayed simply as dots on a computer screen, or in a magazine, it is the thoughts of the mind that become sins affecting the heart.

In the Internet age in which we live, a few keyboard strokes can bring up pornography instantly. This ease of access causes children to be exposed to pornography at a much younger age. Because it is so easy, more children as well as men and women are viewing pornography than ever before.

The use of pornography for sexual stimulation can lead to addiction. Worse, when viewing pornography leads to orgasmic release by masturbation, it can be a further source of demonization. During the act of masturbation, it is possible that a sexual tie can be made to the image on the screen, which needs to be broken with prayer.

Many Christians are caught up in a demonic cycle: First there's a compelling urge to view porn. Next, they succumb to the compulsion. Then, feelings of remorse and regret set in. To many, the power to resist this cycle seems beyond their control. When it is all over, guilt sets in along with self-condemnation for another failure of willpower.

To become free of pornographic addiction, prayer ministry may be needed. After repentance, the evil spirits must be cast out. There must also be the deliberate action of the addicted person to exercise their free will to walk away from pornographic material. The key to a holy life is a Spirit-controlled thought life, but the Holy Spirit will never override anyone's free will. The Spirit of God will not stop the person from falling back into sin again—it's a choice. God will remove the evil spirits driving the compulsion, but the person's lustful desires must be put to death in cooperation with the Holy Spirit to control self-will. Some people seeking freedom who are having a hard time getting victory over pornography check into rehab centers so the viewing cycle can be broken.

A study done by Barna Group gives us some clear facts about the use of pornography by Christians:

21% of youth pastors and 14% of pastors admit they currently struggle with using porn. About 12% of youth pastors and 5% of pastors say they are addicted to porn.

When asked the question, "What makes something porn?" The top two reasons given were:

1. 70%: if it's watched/listened to/or read specifically for the purpose of sexual arousal.

2. 60%: if you masturbated while watching/listening to/or reading it. [1]

Drug and Alcohol Abuse:

Drugs are prevalent in our society, and whether they are prescription or street drugs, many people are using them to feed their addictions. The Greek word for the use of medicine, drugs and spells is *pharmakeia*. The word occurs two times in the New Testament, each of which is in reference to witchcraft or sorcery. [2] Therefore, it only makes sense that a prayer minister needs to understand the effects of drugs because so many people who come for prayer are using them.

Doctors in first-world countries commonly prescribe drugs to treat depression, anxiety and many other mental conditions, with the goal of changing the chemistry of the brain and to alter certain feelings, symptoms or behaviors. With this in mind, I sometimes ask if a person is taking any medications and what type, but for informational purposes only; I never ask someone to reduce their dose or to stop taking a medication. It is very important to remember that prayer ministers are usually not doctors. Even if they are, the person's private physician should always be consulted regarding any medication changes. Sometimes such medications are very good options in a variety of conditions, and while the prayer minister understands that complete healing is possible through the Lord, he or she should never assume or advise that someone should stop their prescription medications.

I ministered to a woman I'll call Jane, who was on medication for over ten years. When she came for prayer with my wife, myself, and some other gifted prayer ministers, she discussed with her husband and her doctor reducing the dose of her medication. Over time, the dose was lowered. One day, some evil spirits manifested, "accusation" being one of them, and changed her behavior dramatically for three days. Then they went back into hiding, and Jane's true personality re-emerged. When Jane realized how she had acted, she apologized to her husband and to the woman she had accused of being her husband's girlfriend. When I asked her if she was going to increase her medication, she said no. Jane and her husband are looking for healing through deliverance, not just behavior modification from drugs. For now, they know from past behavior that in episodes several months apart, the demonic comes forward to control Jane for two to three days and then retreats again for a time. They are willing to live with that pattern until Jane is ready and able to receive more prayer ministry.

Demons may operate in certain parts of the brain, and medication can change the chemistry of the brain, so the demons have a harder time affecting it. Many times, I have heard people say that their brain chemistry is off, which is why they have to take medication. That seems true, but the question to ask is, why is it off? A possible answer is that the demonic is causing a change in their brain chemistry, not always, but sometimes. Remember: nothing is always. After ministry, I have seen people who were diagnosed as bi-polar come off medication to lead normal, healthy lives. It could require many prayer sessions with several different prayer ministers, or it could happen in one two-hour session. The beautiful thing about prayer is that people actually get healed, while medication just masks symptoms. How wonderful that Jesus can, and does, actually heal people.

Street drugs fit into the same biblical category of 'pharmakeia' as prescribed drugs, all of which can open spiritual doors that allow many different spirits to enter. Addiction and paranoia come to mind, but there are undoubtedly many drug-induced spirits with other names. I often talk to people who say that the Bible doesn't say not to use street drugs and that cannabis is now legal in many states for recreational use. Even many Christians are using it now to get high because "after all, it is legal isn't it?" But legality is just an excuse; it's compromise with the world that goes hand-in-hand with the debauchery of which Ephesians 5:18 (NET) speaks:

And do not get drunk with wine, which is debauchery, but be filled by the Spirit...

Debauchery is extreme indulgence in bodily pleasures and especially sexual pleasures: behavior involving sex, drugs, alcohol, etc. that is often considered immoral. [3] The teaching in Ephesians is clear that drunkenness with wine is debauchery, so it is easy in principle to put a teaching together that recreational drugs as an indulgence of bodily pleasures fits well into the definition of debauchery. Though prescription drugs, alcohol and cannabis are legal in secular law, we, as men and women of God, should be seeking the infilling of the Holy Spirit rather than drug-induced fleshly pleasures.

Many experts claim that cannabis in not addictive, but I can testify from personal experience that they are wrong. In my younger years, I used to smoke it and, believe me I was quite addicted. After two years of trying to stop, I decided to sit on a boulder and pray one more time for Jesus to help me quit. Holy Spirit came to help, and even though that was the last time I smoked, there remained a struggle to put my flesh down and to indulge again. After the spirit of addiction was gone, there was still a habit that had been formed in my mind, a behavioral pattern that had to be broken. I had not skied without being high for many years, and my mind would always suggest, "Let's ski high today!"

Anything that keeps the mind focused on the drug, the experience and the feeling of being high is a distraction from God, and therefore becomes an idol. Drugs lead to idolatry and debauchery, just like getting drunk does.

I read the gruesome story below and thought to myself, "What a shame. " I have included it as a teaching about drugs because it is such a clear example of evil accessing the mind through a door opened by *pharmakeia*:[4]

A South Carolina woman who gouged her eyes out in public while in a drug-induced high said she believed the drugs were bringing her closer to God.

Kaylee Muthart, 20, of Anderson, SC, opened up to Cosmopolitan magazine about how she went from a straight-A student occasionally drinking and smoking marijuana to having meth and ecstasy on a regular basis.

She said it all began last summer when she smoked marijuana laced with a narcotic that she believes may have been cocaine or meth. Following the incident, she left school and her job because she felt she was betrayed by the friend who gave her the laced substance.

Soon after Muthart said her relationship with her boyfriend of two years "began to deteriorate" and she smoked marijuana and took Xanax to cope. Their breakup led to a mental breakdown and a bipolar disorder diagnosis.

Muthart said she eventually found a new job but could not shake off the thoughts of how the laced marijuana made her feel. It was those feelings that made her decide to smoke meth last August.

She lost her job because she was "too embarrassed" to go to work after she picked at her face following her trip on the narcotic.

Eventually, Muthart turned to ecstasy as well.
"While on ecstasy, I studied the Bible," Muthart said. "I misinterpreted a lot of it. I convinced myself that meth would bring me even closer to God. "

During Thanksgiving, her mother Katy Tompkins tried to intervene and even recorded a phone conversation between the two of them to get a court order that would force her daughter into a rehab center.

However, Muthart bought meth from her dealer. She recalled that she injected "a larger dose [of meth] that I'd ever used before. "

This was on Feb. 6, 2018. That day, while hallucinating from the large dose, Muthart recalled that she thought, "someone had to sacrifice something important to the world, and that person was me. "

"I thought everything would end abruptly, and everyone would die, if I didn't tear out my eyes immediately," she said. " I don't know how I came to that conclusion, but I felt it was, without doubt, the right, rational thing to do immediately. "

Muthart said the man she had been staying with, who she did not identify but said had a biblical name, was driving by and asked her a question. She said she felt that the encounter was her sign.

What happened next has left Muthart completely blind. "So, I pushed my thumb, pointer, and middle finger into each eye. I gripped each eyeball, twisted, and pulled until each eye popped out of the socket — it felt like a massive struggle, the hardest thing I ever had to do," she said. "Because I could no longer see, I don't know if there was blood. But I know the drugs numbed the pain. I'm pretty sure I would have tried to claw right into my brain if a pastor hadn't heard me screaming, 'I want to see the light!' — which I don't recall saying — and restrained me. "

She continued: "He later said, when he found me, that I was holding my eyeballs in my hands. I had squished them, although they were somehow still attached to my head. "

Across the street, terrified churchgoers from the South Main Chapel and Mercy Center watched on.

Muthart said that during the incident her mother was traveling to the courthouse to get her committed to the rehabilitation center but "she was too late. "

Following her surgery to save her optic nerves, Muthart said she "knew" she was blind and suffered from bad headaches. She said she refused powerful painkillers despite her pain and even asked visitors to describe how she looked now that she could not see.

Since then, Muthart has been clean. She has been adapting to her new lifestyle and hoped to go back to school for marine biology. She also plans to attend 90 Narcotics Anonymous meetings and hopes to raise enough money on GoFundMe for a seeing-eye dog.

Despite the situation, Muthart said she is "happier now than she was before all this happened. " "I'd rather be blind than dependent on drugs," she said. "It took losing my sight to get me back on the right path, but from the bottom of my heart, I'm so glad I'm here."

We can see in this tragic story that the mind was opened to evil influence by the drugs. The writer stated, her breakup with her boyfriend "led to a mental breakdown and a bipolar disorder diagnosis. " The trigger for the mental illness to manifest was the drugs and the breakup. While the mental breakdown and bipolar disorder were triggered by the trauma of the breakup, I believe the problem was actually caused by demonization. Remember, while hallucinating from the large dose, Muthart recalled that she thought, "Someone had to sacrifice something important to the world, and that person was me. " It seems apparent that the drugs opened her mind to receive the suggestion, the thought, from the demonic. It wasn't her own thought; she only believed it was, saying, "I thought everything would end abruptly, and everyone would die, if I didn't tear out my eyes immediately. I don't know how I came to that conclusion, but I felt it was, without doubt, the right, rational thing to do immediately. " I can tell you how she came to that conclusion; evil was accessing her mind because it was left unguarded and was wide open to the spirit realm because of the meth she had injected.

It is not just methamphetamine that can open the mind to the spirit ream. LSD, mushrooms, peyote, ketamine, ecstasy, and many of the new designer drugs can also open the mind to evil influence; some are even used during rituals in order to achieve contact with spirits.

Eating Disorders:

Certainly, nobody sets out to suffer from an eating disorder, which is an addictive behavior. Regardless of however, it happens, whether through generational or personal sin or through various traumatic events, demonic rights have been obtained. Sadly, it is often our society that sets up such unrealistic expectations of beauty that some young girls get trapped in vicious cycles of demonically controlled overeating behaviors just because they want to fit in and be accepted by others.

Anorexia occurs when a person stops eating enough food to sustain a healthy body. They look at themselves in a mirror and appear over-weight in their own eyes. Really, they are quite thin, but the demon affects how they see and think. I believe that the person is looking through the eyes of the demon, so they see themselves as overweight. Severe anorexia can lead to death, which is an end that any demon would be proud to cause.

Bulimia occurs when a person eats and then forcefully vomits up the meal in order to avoid gaining weight, a behavior that is commonly known as binging and purging. Not only is the stomach acid quite bad for the esophagus and tooth enamel, but since the food never passes through the digestive system, bulimia can cause serious nutritional deficiencies. Like anorexia, there is a demon behind bulimia, which drives the compulsive behavior.

Overeating is another issue, referred to as gluttony in the Bible:

Hear, my son, and be wise; And guide your heart in the way. Do not mix with winebibbers, Or with gluttonous eaters of meat; For the drunkard and the glutton will come to poverty, And drowsiness will clothe a man with rags. (Proverbs 23:19-21)

Regardless of whether an addiction is related to issues of sex, alcohol, drugs, food or anything else, demonization is an underlying problem and Jesus is the Deliverer.

CHAPTER 15

AT THE HANDS OF OTHERS

W e'll now consider some of the specific actions of others that put us in danger.

Abuse and Rejection:

Physical and/or verbal abuse and rejection are sins against others. Although the abuser is the one committing the sin, the abuse recipient can become demonized. Whether a young child or an adult, we all crave love, affection and care. When that is withheld, a lack of freedom may result.

Anne and I recently ministered to a young woman who felt on the verge of a 'nervous breakdown'. While she was growing up, her mom had been telling her she was stupid. This traumatic verbal abuse caused a stronghold, or trigger, to be established in her mind. Now as an adult, a person at work was calling her stupid, which triggered feelings from her childhood that sent her into a state of panic and anxiety. We first led her in a prayer to forgive her mother and asked the Lord to heal the stronghold in her mind. We then instructed her to create a boundary with the abuser at her workplace. The man who was telling her she was stupid *and* the demon that inspired his words, had to be told firmly that she will not allow him to speak to her that way any longer.

Either excessive spanking or excessive discipline are areas of great concern; and verbal abuse can be just as damaging as that which is physical.

In the Womb:

Trauma during pregnancy can lead to demonization. Fighting and arguing between parents is a set-up for the spirit of rejection to enter. The mother's thinking or saying things like, "What am I going to do?" or "I wish I wasn't pregnant," creates an unhealthy environment for a developing child. The spirit of rejection can enter a child while still in the womb in this type of situation. Also, if either parent is considering abortion, this can lead to evil spirits such as rejection, death and worthlessness plaguing the child. The act of abortion can open doors to demonization of the parents too.

Curses and Witchcraft

Curses are evil words spoken with intent to harm someone. Also, they can be words of criticism or condemnation verbalized to or about someone, even if they were not intended to harm but to correct. The power of our words can open a legal right for evil to attach to the person who has been criticized. Believing or receiving any false truths spoken to us can greatly affect us.

People often speak curses over themselves too, unintentionally and unknowingly setting evil into motion within their own lives. Randy Clark's book, *The Biblical Guidebook to Deliverance,* includes an excellent teaching about curses and witchcraft:[1]

https://www.amazon.com/dp/B00U58QKJM

In Brazil, my friend Tom Hauser was touched one night by the power of the Holy Spirit. Authority over the demonic realm was given to him as we prayed over him. Hauser received a powerful fresh baptism of the Holy Spirit that resulted in a strong gift of discerning of spirits and authority for the ministry of deliverance. At the service that evening was a woman named June whose right leg was turned a full ninety degrees out toward the right. As Tom interviewed her, he found out that before June was born, her parents had a neighbor whose daughter's leg was also turned ninety degrees toward the right. June's father had mocked and derided the neighbor's child, causing the neighbor to speak a curse over June's mother when she was pregnant with June. When June was born, she had the same deformity.

The neighbor who spoke the curse was involved in Macumba witchcraft. I believe it was this curse that brought an evil spirit upon the mother and June, while she was unborn, causing the deformity of her leg. As Tom ministered deliverance, which was a process that took two nights, those of us on the team watched the foot and leg turn, eighty degrees the first night and the remaining ten degrees the second night. All of the bones moved; everything shifted. As the demonic spirit was dealt with, the curse was broken, and June was healed.

Ritual and/or Sexual Abuse:

I ministered to a woman who was abused in satanic rituals in the Church of Satan. Her mother took her to be used in the rituals when she was a baby, and sexual abuse was part of the ceremonies. Such ritual abuse always opens doors for demons.

If the abuse starts at a very young age, the person often develops Dissociative Identity Disorder or DID, formerly recognized as Multiple Personality Disorder. During the abuse, a detaching or dissociating occurs as a survival mechanism to remove oneself from the pain and horror. It is quite complex to minister to someone with D. I. D. because there can be many personalities residing in them, including both male and female parts. Also, one personality might be a Christian, while another could deny Christ. Until you can discover whom the primary or original personality is, it can be quite confusing. To make things even more complicated, there are also demons involved. One way to test if you are dealing with one type if dissociation is to ask the person if they lose time. When one personality is presenting, the others often don't know what is happening or how long they have been in the background. When the next personality comes forward, he or she might look at their watch and wonder what has been happening. If one personality stays forward long enough, hours, days, or even longer periods of time may be lost.

Laying on of Hands:

The laying on of hands can be a powerful spiritual experience because a supernatural exchange of power, either for good or evil, can be released from one person to another. Normally, the power flows from the one laying on hands to the one who receives what is being given, but sometimes it can also flow the other way. We have noticed that it is best when casting out demons not to lay hands on the person because evil can get back onto your hands causing an evil tingling, known as 'poison,' in the deliverance world. When we have had this happen, we ask the Lord to clean off our hands and the tingling goes away.

Ruth Prince, Derrick's wife, offers a good teaching that illustrates this danger of laying hands on another in his book, *They Shall Expel Demons*:[2]

https://www.amazon.com/dp/0800792602

In 1971, I was attending a charismatic meeting, and the speaker asked people to stand if they wanted prayer for healing. I had a bad cold, so I stood. He then instructed people seated nearby to lay their hands on us and pray for our healing. Four or five prayed for me.

When I awoke the next morning, my cold was better, but my fingers were all curled up and stiff and hurting. Immediately I thought, "Someone with arthritis laid hands on me last night!" I renounced the spirit of arthritis, and within five minutes all the symptoms were gone.

When praying for someone, it is very important to always ask permission if you want to touch him or her. Also, when someone wants to touch you, be very cautious, especially if you don't know the person. When in doubt, say no.

CHAPTER 16
SEX & DEMONIZATION

Discussion of sex and demonization is often not something that most Christians want to explore. Regardless, a book about deliverance must include the subject because sex is often used as a demonic tool to open doors into people. Also, demons use people to have perverted sexual encounters with other demons. The subject must be discussed and understood if we are to be effective prayer ministers.

Sexual Abuse:

Sexual encounters are spiritual in nature and there is no ungodly sexual contact that is without negative spiritual consequences. Whenever any level of sexual abuse has occurred, there is likely to be demonization, even if there was only one seemingly mild and long-forgotten encounter from childhood: the memory of the event could be buried deep in the mind and repressed. Sexual demons that entered during the event can warp the sexual desires for children as they reach puberty, or even before, manifesting in a dysfunctional sexual appetite. For example, sex could become either despised or craved. Later, if there is a marriage relationship, the demons will do all they can to interfere with the sexual function and satisfaction, and a lack of intimacy in the martial bed could destroy the marriage.

Some sexual demons appear to believe that they own the inhabited person sexually and don't want to share them with the spouse, prompting behaviors or excuses to avoid intimacy. I ministered to a woman with this type of demon, and almost every time before she and her husband were about to become intimate, the spirit would cause her to criticize the man, resulting in an argument and preventing the union. This cycle continued for over twenty years, until she received prayer ministry and was delivered of the evil spirit, which finally enabled this couple to enjoy wonderful times of sexual intimacy. One name for this demon is Asmodeus.

Couples seeking help from secular counselors can become even more demonized, because they may recommend using pornography, perverted sex or the use of sex toys to enhance a relationship. Attempts to heal the relationship with fleshly fixes will never work. Unless the person who was sexually abused gets deliverance ministry or, better yet, both husband and wife do, there will be little improvement. Over time they will have to settle for an inadequate sexual relationship, and many end up separated or divorced due to a lack of a healthy sexual relationship.

Sexual Promiscuity:

Any sex outside of a marriage covenant is sin; it can both open doors to demonization and create ungodly spiritual ties to the sexual partner because they become one flesh. In the United States, condoms are distributed in middle school, and kids are told that if they feel attracted to someone, it is fine to follow their feelings. They are also taught that same-sex homosexual attractions are acceptable, because the educators have no idea what the spiritual consequences of sex outside of marriage are. The casual sexual encounters that are condoned can lead to homosexual and/or other unrighteous sexual spirits entering the children, perverting their desires for intimacy with either the same or opposite sex.

But from the beginning of the creation, God made them male and female. For this reason a man shall leave his father and mother and be joined to his wife, and the two shall become one flesh; so then they are no longer two, but one flesh. (Mark 10:6-10)

The sin of sex out of wedlock can also cause fragments of the person's soul to be stuck in other dimensions. Spiritual ties that have been created need to be broken through repentance and prayer and the fragments need to be recovered through prayer.

...but if you return to Me, and keep My commandments and do them, though some of you were cast out to the farthest part of the heavens, yet I will gather them from there, and bring them to the place which I have chosen as a dwelling for My name. (Nehemiah 1:9)

Male Microchimerism:

According to the below article, women absorb and retain DNA from every man they have sex with. If this is true, then it would explain a physical tie between sexual partners. A literal physical mingling of the flesh could occur. [1]

Women retain and carry living DNA from every man with whom they have sexual intercourse, according to a new study by the University of Seattle and the Fred Hutchinson Cancer Research Center.

The study, which discovered the startling information by accident, was originally trying to determine if women who have been pregnant with a son might be more predisposed to certain neurological diseases that occur more frequently in males.

But as the scientists picked apart the female brain, the study began to veer wildly off course. As it turns out, the female brain is even more mysterious than we previously thought.

The study found that female brains often harbor "male microchimerism", in other words, the presence of male DNA that originated from another individual and are genetically distinct from the cells that make up the rest of the woman.

According to the study: "63% of the females (37 of 59) tested harbored male microchimerism in the brain. Male microchimerism was present in multiple brain regions. "

So, 63% of those women carry male DNA cells that live in their brains. Obviously, the researchers wanted to know where the male DNA came from.

Anyone care to guess? From the women's fathers? No. Your father's DNA combines with your mothers to create your unique DNA. So, where else could it come from?

Through the study the researchers assumed that the most likely answer was that all male DNA found living in the female brain came from a male pregnancy. That was the safe, politically correct assumption. But, these researchers were living in denial, because when they autopsied the brains of women who had never even been pregnant, let alone with a male child, they STILL found male DNA cells prevalent in the female brain.

At this point the scientists didn't know what was going on. Confused, they did their best to hide the evidence until they could understand and explain it. They buried it in numerous sub studies and articles. When you sift through them all, however, you will find the damning statement, the one line that gives the game away and explains exactly where these male DNA cells come from.

What are they so afraid of?

"CONCLUSIONS: Male microchimerism was not infrequent in women without sons. Besides known pregnancies, other possible sources of male microchimerism include unrecognized spontaneous abortion, vanished male twin, an older brother transferred by the maternal circulation, or SEXUAL INTER-COURSE. Male microchimerism was significantly more frequent and levels were higher in women with induced abortion than in women with other pregnancy histories. Further studies are needed to determine specific origins of male microchimerism in women. "

According to the scientists, then, the possible sources of the male DNA cells living in the women's brains are:

1. An abortion the woman didn't know about
2. A male twin that vanished
3. An older brother transferred by the maternal circulation
4. Sexual intercourse

Considering the fact that 63% of women have male DNA cells residing in the recesses of their brain, which of the above possibilities do you think is the most likely origin of the male DNA?

The first three options apply to a very small percentage of women. They couldn't possibly account for the 63% figure. The fourth option? It's rather more common. The answer is 4: Sex.

This has very important ramifications for women. Every male whose spermatozoa you absorb becomes a living part of you for life. The women autopsied in this study were elderly. Some had been carrying the living male DNA inside them for well over 50 years.

Sperm is alive. It is living cells. When it is injected into you, it swims and swims until it crashes headlong into a wall. Then it attaches and burrows into your flesh. If it's in your mouth, it swims and climbs into your nasal passages, inner ear, and behind your eyes, where it digs in. It enters your blood stream and collects in your brain and spine. Like something out of a sci-fi movie, it becomes a part of you, and you can't get rid of it.

We are only now beginning to understand the full power and ramifications of sexual intercourse.

Premarital Intercourse:

Premarital intercourse is very common is our society. There is a belief that since couples are going to be married anyway, there should be no spiritual consequences. There is also the belief that marriage is old fashioned and no longer necessary, but all sex outside of marriage is sin and can open one up to demonization.

Peter Horrobin tells about a woman he ministered to who had premarital intercourse:[2]

> One person who confessed that she and her husband had commenced sexual relations together three months before they got married (neither of them had ever had sex with any other person before or after marriage) had become an epileptic shortly after they married. We did not know this when we first ministered to her. But she heard and understood the teaching and wanted to put it right before God. Immediately [when] she confessed the sin, the ungodly dimension to the soul tie with her husband was broken and the powers of darkness were commanded to leave. As she did, she collapsed and manifested all the symptoms of having a grand mal epileptic seizure on our meeting room floor.

> Ten minutes later she had a second fit, but then she got up off the floor, claiming to have been completely healed. We asked her why she said that. She told us that she was on the highest possible safe dosage of anti-epileptic drugs allowed and still she had many seizures. Every time she had a seizure it would normally take two to three days in a darkened room to recover from the pain, the trauma and the flashing lights. But after two seizures in the course of her prayer ministry, she got up immediately and felt great.

> Three years later she wrote telling us how she had come off all her anti-epileptic drugs (in cooperation with her local doctor) within a matter of weeks. Since then, she has had no further seizures and has not been on any medication either. In her case, the sexual sin had opened up a demonic doorway for two spirits of infirmity causing epilepsy to come into her, and as soon as

her relationship (which had become ungodly) was consecrated before God in marriage, the condition began to manifest itself.

I doubt if the spirits of epilepsy would have manifested at all if she had decided to continue in a promiscuous lifestyle with other people.

Christians really need to have their minds made up not to give in to strong sexual urges that develop when two people are dating and in love. By no means am I saying that a spirit of epilepsy will come onto all that have premarital sex, but there are always consequences to sin. I have included this story as an interesting example of how the sin of premarital intercourse can open unexpected doors and lead to serious problems.

Sex toys:

God designed us to satisfy each other without bringing devices into our times of intimacy. The Bible teaches that married couples are to have sex with each other. Bringing a machine into the bedroom could be considered like bringing in a third party; even though it is only a machine, it is a third element in bed besides you and your spouse. Addiction to sex toys is real, and using them can lead to a lack of satisfaction during intercourse when they are not used.

Adultery:

Adultery is quite an obvious doorway to defilement of the wedding bed. The marriage vows taken before God create a covenant relationship between husband and wife. Even if God was not acknowledged during the wedding, the signing of the marriage document created a legal covenant. When broken, that sin gives the right for demons to enter. During an adulterous affair, evil spirits can be picked up, brought home, and transferred to the spouse. Also, unwanted pregnancy and sexual transmitted diseases are a grim reality.

As mentioned before, pornography is also a form of adultery, and even more so if a person masturbates while viewing it. That type of fantasy sex can create an evil spiritual tie to the person viewed in the pornography.

Sex with demons:

In Zambia, it is common for people to have 'spirit wives' or 'spirit husbands. These are demons that come during the night to have sex with a human. The sex can be quite enjoyable, so people go along with it for the pleasure they receive. When sharing what happens in these encounters, they often explain that the demon can pleasure them more than a human. Aside from the fact that evil uses the person for sexual pleasure, there is another problem; I have read about demons coming every night for years, tormenting the person and preventing a good night's sleep. Sometimes it is a violent event with the demon raping the man or woman. I have also read accounts about demons physically penetrating the man or woman.

While in Africa, a friend from our ministry team was staying in a hotel one night after he preached. A female looking spirit came into his room and lay down on him. He explained that it was quite arousing, and he began to have sex with it, but once he realized what was happening, he commanded it to leave and it did. The next day when he told me what happened, I was quite concerned and stated he could have become tied to it spiritually had he finished the sex act. These kinds of events seem to be more prevalent in Africa, but I know people in the United States that have had the same thing happen to them.

The testimony of a former Mormon described her demonic sexual encounter:[3]

I was raised in a devout Mormon family and. . . had experienced a few times, the "witness of the holy ghost" (aka bosom burning) that is so common in Mormonism. But because of unanswered questions that troubled me so much about that faith, I went through a 10-year period of deprogramming, during which the Lord penetrated my heart with the pure, simple, beautiful message of Christianity. I gave my life to Christ early this year. I had always thought of myself as a Christian but I wasn't reading my Bible or truly trusting God until this awakening...[I'd] prayed as [I] typically did up until then, for this "witness of the holy ghost"...I wanted a sign from above to confirm that God was with me, that he loved me and approved of my choices. One nagging prayer was repeated – that God would reveal for me the reason why my Mormon friends and family do in fact receive the witness of the holy ghost, to confirm the divinity of the Book of Mormon, if in fact, it wasn't of God at all. I didn't yet understand that this type of prayer was unbiblical and left-over Mormonism. The spirit came, the same bosom burning, loving/beautiful feeling, beyond any explanation.

Pure love. . . after I praised and welcomed it, this very real person/spirit purposely and forcefully sexually aroused me, followed by unearthly sexual pleasure.

It repeatedly lied and claimed to be God, seeking my love and worship and praise. It would grow warmer and stronger when I would praise it. For 4 days I bounced between praising it and demanding it out in the name of Jesus Christ. Although it was very convincing that it had to be God, I knew that it was unbiblical, as it clearly did not wish for me to read my bible or take care of my responsibilities – it simply wanted me to be alone, put my head back and commune with it as it moved through me in an almost tangible way, over and over. When I finally decided to completely ignore it altogether and solely focus my thoughts on Jesus, it left in a dramatic way, causing me to cough violently. As it left, I felt light (it had made me feel slow and heavy) and scriptural knowledge was poured into me quickly "of course that was not me, but the God of the Book of Mormon, who you ask for.

"It is gone and has no legal right to return to you, I am with you. Do not seek signs or feelings because they are deceiving, my love for you is confirmed in the scriptures and my Word is sufficient. Testify of this devil to the Mormons that you know".

"I know that there are many Christian scholars who teach that what I experienced as a Christian is impossible. But it happened. I don't know if a Christian who had not been involved in the occult could have a devil enter them or not. My Lord never abandoned me, I invited this deceptive angel of light and God, in his glory, used this awful, invasive experience to give me my answer, the testimony... Satan is real, he is crafty and can appear more beautiful than any earthly person. He is a liar and I can't emphasize enough that he hates Christians and our witnessing, our coming to the light and sharing it with others. It is a very personal war and he tells us that we are insignificant but in truth, our testimonies are a terrific threat to the devil. Don't keep quiet!"

Clearly, the Christian walk can be corrupted by demonic sexual encounters. A good generational prayer to deal with this is *The Prayer to Break all Ties to the Incubus and Succubus Spirit.* [4]

Bestiality:

In Northern Columbia, it is culturally acceptable for boys and men to have sex with donkeys That isn't something that is common in our society, but men having sex with various animals does happen here, and bestial sexual activity is often forced upon women. Such a lady who wanted healing contacted a prayer minister friend; she had been forced by her husband to have sex with a dog. In South Africa, witch doctors (sangomas) insert snakes into women to increase fertility. Scripture is clear that there are severe consequences to such forbidden actions:

> *If a man mates with an animal, he shall surely be put to death, and you shall kill the animal. If a woman approaches any animal and mates with it, you shall kill the woman and the animal. They shall surely be put to death. Their blood is upon them.* (Leviticus 20:15-16)

Whoever lies with an animal shall surely be put to death. (Exodus 22:19)

Biblically, the punishment for man, woman and animal was death. I believe that God chose that punishment so that the generational curse would not be passed down the generational line. We need to be thankful that Jesus has brought the ministry of deliverance to us. Through His blood we can repent and have the consequences of our sin removed, allowing us to walk in His wonderful freedom.

Anal Sex:

Peter Horrobin writes:[5]

God designed man and woman to be able to have intercourse by the insertion of the male sexual organ into the female one. Subsequent orgasm is a source of intense pleasure for both part-ners and the ejaculation of the sperm into the female is the means of fertilizing the eggs so that reproduction may occur. Ejaculation of the sperm into any other orifice is a perversion of what God planned and purposed for mankind.

We have found that when people, married or not, have indulged in such perverted sex, demons with a similarly perverted character have also entered. The consequences have been everything from physical infirmities in and around the organs involved, often of a medically un-diagnosable nature, to an increasingly lustful desire for more and more perverted sex.

The natural use of the anus is an outlet for feces, not a sexual orifice, and anal sex exposes a person to significant risk of infection caused by bacteria.

Some believe that Old Testament references to sodomy refer to men lying with men, with 'sodomy' meaning 'unnatural sexual inter-course'. In the Bible, sodomites refer to male homosexuals or temple prostitutes (both male and female). But the New Testament also speaks about sodomy:

> *Do you not know that the unrighteous will not inherit the kingdom of God? Do not be deceived. Neither fornicators, nor idolaters, nor adulterers, nor homosexuals, nor sodomites, nor thieves, nor covetous, nor drunkards, nor revilers, nor extortioners will inherit the kingdom of God.* (1 Corinthians 6:9-10)

> *...knowing this: that the law is not made for a righteous person, but for the lawless and insubordinate, for the ungodly and for sinners, for the unholy and profane, for murderers of fathers and murderers of mothers, for manslayers, for fornicators, for sodomites, for kidnappers, for liars, for perjurers, and if there is any other thing that is contrary to sound doctrine, according to the glorious gospel of the blessed God which was committed to my trust.* (1 Timothy 1:9-12)

Clearly, God does not approve of such actions!

Homosexuality, lesbianism, transvestism and trans-sexuality:

The homosexual lifestyle is forbidden in Scripture in both the Old and New Testaments. No amount of reinterpretation to make it acceptable in our current culture can make it acceptable before God. It is clear that such things are forbidden.

> *You shall not lie with a male as with a woman. It is an abomination.* (Leviticus18:22)

> *For this reason, God gave them up to vile passions. For even their women exchanged the natural use for what is against nature. Likewise, also the men, leaving the natural use of the woman, burned in their lust for one another, men with men committing what is shameful, and receiving in themselves the penalty of their error which was due. And even as they did not like to retain God in their knowledge, God gave them over to a debased mind, to do those things which are not fitting;*

being filled with all unrighteousness, sexual immorality, wickedness, covetousness, maliciousness; full of envy, murder, strife, deceit, evil-mindedness; they are whisperers, backbiters, haters of God, violent, proud, boasters, inventors of evil things, disobedient to parents, undiscerning, untrustworthy, unloving, unforgiving, unmerciful; who, knowing the righteous judgment of God, that those who practice such things are deserving of death, not only do the same but also approve of those who practice them. (Romans 1:26-32)

Unclean spirits drive homosexuality, and the name of one such spirit that causes homosexuality is Gaia, also spelled Gaea. This spirit, which can also afflict heterosexual and bi-sexual people, can also tempt people to indulge in pornography.

Wiktionary defines a transvestite as:

A person who sometimes wears clothes traditionally worn by and associated with the opposite sex, typically a male who cross-dresses occasionally by habit or compulsion. [6]

Dressing in clothing of the opposite sex should be not be encouraged by parents as it could encourage or lead to transvestism.

Merriam-Webster defines transsexual as:

Relating to or being a person whose gender identity is opposite the sex the person had or was identified as having at birth. [7]

Transsexual people may or may not undergo surgery and hormone therapy to obtain the physical appearance typical of the gender with which they identify. Even worse, these days our society encourages everyone, including small children, that they can choose to select their gender. Society often prosecutes anyone who dares to disagree. The end result is demonic chaos and confusion.

CHAPTER 17
THE UNDEFILED MARRIAGE BED

The Bible is clear that the sanctity of the marriage bed is critical:

Marriage must be honored among all and the marriage bed kept unde-filed, for God will judge sexually immoral people and adulterers. (Hebrews 13:4-25 NET)

A couple of interesting questions are:

- What is acceptable sexual behavior for the Christian bedroom, and what kind of behavior would be defiling?
- What does God prohibit in the sexual relationship between a husband and wife, and what does he permit?

As I began to study this controversial subject it was apparent that God gives tremendous sexual freedom within the marriage relationship. Discussing the subject with select, educated Christian friends, it became obvious that people have various opinions about what is acceptable and what isn't.

The law of love in Romans is a good place to start to answer these interesting questions:

I know and am convinced by the Lord Jesus that there is nothing unclean itself; but to him who considers anything to be unclean, to him it is unclean. (Romans 14:14)

We may wish to try something new in bed and find that our spouse is uncomfortable trying it, so to him or her it is unclean and should not be pursued. Repeatedly pressuring a spouse to do something they don't want to do sexually because we are trying to get what we want regardless of their feelings enables ungodly spirits of control, or even witchcraft. What one couple considers acceptable can be considered degrading by another, so in order to know what is acceptable we must ask the Holy Spirit to come into the bedroom with us; He will show us what is OK and what that is not. Conviction of something we are doing that is not pleasing to the Holy Spirit should be acknowledged and heeded. Remember, He said that He will write His laws on our hearts.

One teaching that is biblically obvious is that anal sex is defiling and should be avoided. Clearly, the natural design of men and women is that the penis is meant to enter the vagina, resulting in orgasm from stimulation of the clitoris and the vagina. This is how God created us; this is His natural design for us. Romans 1:26-27 refers to the Greek *phusikos* as 'natural use'.

For this reason, God gave them up to vile passions. For even their women exchanged the natural use for what is against nature. Likewise, also the men, leaving the natural use of the woman, burned in their lust for one another, men with men committing what is shameful, and receiving in themselves the penalty of their error which was due.

Strong's Concordance states:[1]

phusikos: natural, according to nature
Original Word: φυσικός, ή, όν
Part of Speech: Adjective
Transliteration: *phusikos*
Phonetic Spelling: (foo-see-kos')

Short Definition: natural, according to nature
Definition: natural, (a) according to nature, (b) merely animal.
Romans 1:26 Adj-AFS
GRK: μετήλλαξαν τὴν φυσικὴν χρῆσιν εἰς
NAS: exchanged the natural function
KJV: women did change the natural use into
INT: changed the natural use into
Romans 1:27 Adj-AFS
GRK: ἀφέντες τὴν φυσικὴν χρῆσιν τῆς
NAS: abandoned the natural function
KJV: leaving the natural use
INT: having left the natural use of the

Apostle Paul chose the Greek word *phusikos* to clearly teach that leaving the natural for the unnatural is unacceptable. Although we normally read this scripture and apply it to homosexuality, we can also apply the principle to the marriage bed. What is acceptable would be natural, and what is not would be unnatural.

When a couple is always looking for a more exciting sexual experience, they can set themselves up to get off track spiritually. Always expecting an ever-more-powerful and longer lasting orgasm is a mindset that can lead to defilement of the marriage bed, and then to demonization.

The transfer of DNA to create a child is, of course, important but it is not the only reason God created sexual intimacy. God designed the marriage bed to be a place where a couple comes together in loving intimacy, a time where the cares and busyness of the world are put on hold so they can simply enjoy each other. The question should not be, "What can I get?" but rather, "What can I give?" It is this giving and receiving pleasure that brings a couple into sexual unity, pleasure and release, and it creates an intimate spiritual bond. Designed by God, it is a gift to us, a time to be cherished and honored and enjoyed.

CHAPTER 18
SEXUAL RESPONSIBILITY IN MARRIAGE

Remember that Satan's job description is to kill, steal and destroy, and since marriage was invented by God and is valued by Him, by default Satan hates it. In fact, whatever is good in the eyes of God, Satan hates; he and his minions target Christian marriages, and blocking sexual intimacy is one of the strategies. Married couples must make it a priority to set aside time together for intimacy. The Bible teaches that our bodies are a gift to our spouse, and we do not have the right to withhold our affections from one another:

> *A husband should give to his wife her sexual rights, and likewise a wife to her husband. It is not the wife who has the rights to her own body, but the husband. In the same way, it is not the husband who has the rights to his own body, but the wife. Do not deprive each other, except by mutual agreement for a specified time, so that you may devote yourselves to prayer. Then resume your relationship, so that Satan may not tempt you because of your lack of self-control.* (1 Corinthians 7:3-5 NET)

A legitimate excuse to deny sex to your spouse occurs if a specified, agreed-upon time has been set aside for prayer and fasting. The above scripture in the NKJV says:

Do not deprive one another except with consent for a time, that you may give yourselves to fasting and prayer; and come together again so that Satan does not tempt you because of your lack of self-control.

All couples can get very busy and fail to leave time for intimacy. For example, a mother of three small children under the age of six is busy all day and usually exhausted by bedtime; she may be very tired, and the last thing she might want to do is to serve her husband's sexual needs. But as we can see in this scripture, we do not have a right to our own body, and we are to give and not deprive each other. The command is clear, *Do not deprive each other.* God created the sexual desires of husband-for-wife and wife-for-husband, so it should never seem as if one is doing a favor for the other; the best you can do at the time is better than denying your spouse.

God gave us the gift of sexual need, and we should be thankful for it; we should celebrate it as a wonderful gift designed not only for personal pleasure, but also to bond a couple together as they each give pleasure to each other. When we can understand this principle, not looking at it as a 'wifely duty' or 'husbandly duty' but as an act that brings them together, the relationship will be blessed with intimate loving closeness.

Linda Dillow and Lorraine Pintus have written:

The only reason Scripture gives for abstaining from frequent sexual encounters is prayer. We've heard a myriad of reasons why women don't want to have sex, but prayer is not on their lists. According to this verse, if we refuse to make love for other reasons, we open our marriage to satanic temptations. As has been said, the Creator who gave us our sexual desire knows this, so He instructs us to participate actively and regularly in sex with our mate. Biblically, sex is not a debatable issue. It is an integral part of marriage.

Some of you may be thinking, Linda and Lorraine, is Scripture saying I can never say "not tonight?" No, but we would caution you to be very careful about how you say it. Men are very vulnerable in the sexual area. You may think women are sensitive in this area, but men are even more sensitive. Remember, their feelings about their masculinity are wrapped up in their prowess as a lover. Your husband feels emotionally rejected when you turn down his sexual advances. It is important that wives understand the vulnerability a man has in offering himself to her.

Yes, there are ways to lovingly say "later" or "for now, let me satisfy you," but we must remember that God says we are to give our bodies as a gift. Perhaps you think that since we are writing a book on sex, both of us are always ready and eager to make love. Not so. Like you, we get tired. We have wacko hormones. We often have "more important" things on our minds. Sometimes we find ourselves irritated with our husbands and don't want to be in the same room with them, let alone the same bed. But we've made a commitment to honor God and be exciting lovers to our husbands. That decision helps our attitudes when sex is the last thing on our minds.

Making the right decision is never easy but there are benefits to adopting the right attitude. When we choose to love selflessly, we honor God, we make our husbands happy, and we find more pleasure in our lovemaking. Dying to self is difficult, but it is necessary if you want to grow in godliness. Being godly means having a godly attitude. Godly attitudes result in godly actions, such as giving your body to your husband. This is easier if you surrender to God and allow His Spirit to work within you. "Nothing is impossible with God" (Luke 1:37 NIV). He is able to give you desire where none existed before. He can help you exchange wrong thinking with godly thinking. He can cause you to enjoy deeper intimacy than you ever thought possible. [1]

Who knows how many marriages Satan has destroyed because a wife was too busy to have sex with her husband? But it does go both ways! I had a close friend whose husband refused to have sex with her, which was one of several reasons the marriage ended in divorce.

When you are too busy or think that something is more important than loving your spouse, that thought should be taken captive. Ask, "Why am I to busy, and what is behind my thinking, that I need to deny my husband or wife?" It could be that demons are influencing your mind and you are not really that busy; it is just evil making you think that you are. I have seen this in ministry sessions; in one case the demons were deceiving a woman into thinking that everything was more important than sex with her husband, trying to destroy the marriage by denying sex to the husband. After deliverance prayer, the excuses not to have sex were gone and the couple entered into a beautiful time of intimacy.

122

CHAPTER 19
THE DECEIVED CHURCH

Oh, how I grieve for the church. But why? They are going to heaven; they are the Bride of Christ and are going to spend eternity with Him. That sounds really good, doesn't it? So why should I grieve? It's because both healing and deliverance are available to the Church by the power of Jesus' sacrifice on the cross, but many don't understand how to appropriate it; they don't understand how to get it though it is right there in front of them. Either they are uninformed and don't know, or else do not believe it is needed.

I try to teach people how to receive healing through deliverance, but so many can't seem to grasp it. For the most part, evil has blinded the church to healing that comes from deliverance. They can't imagine that evil could be affecting them because, after all, they are covered in the blood of Jesus and the blood breaks all curses and sets us free, doesn't it? That is what they say, and they are right – to an extent, What they don't understand is this simple but powerful truth: We can be healed and delivered, with generational curses broken; but it is not automatic for these things to occur. We must appropriate it. Yes, it is available, but I'll say it again, we must appropriate it. We must come to the Lord in repentance and humility to ask for our healing from demonic influence in each instance that is revealed. This is the way He operates; this is what He is waiting for. He wants His bride to be pure and spotless, and this is how it happens; this is how we work out our salvation with fear and trembling. [1]

As has been stated, sometimes automatic or sovereign deliverance and healing may occur after salvation. Still, for the most part, we must come to Him over time. I'm certain that when the Holy Spirit comes into someone, some demons freak out and leave in fear of His presence, but it is obvious that all of them don't go. There are evil generational rights. If you believe they are all broken when the Holy Spirit comes in, you are believing a lie. That is exactly what the devil wants you to believe so you will remain bound by evil generational rights. Jesus said:

> *Come to Me, all you who labor and are heavy laden, and I will give you rest. Take My yoke upon you and learn from Me, for I am gentle and lowly in heart, and you will find rest for your souls. For My yoke is easy and My burden is light.* (Matthew 11:28-30)

A pastor friend who had graduated from seminary many years before, sat with me at a Starbucks for a couple of hours after I had the revelation download in Rock Creek Canyon. I shared in detail how the demons had come out of me after being in the church for seventeen years. Before that my logic had been that if I attended church faithfully and went to all the Bible studies, home groups, and seminars, I would be free; yet, I didn't get delivered. Was I any different from him? Did I have more generational curses and demons than other people in the church? I did some things before I got saved that allowed evil to affect me, but was I that much different from anyone else?

My pastor friend just couldn't imagine that he might not be completely free from evil. He argued adamantly that demons just come out after you are saved because they can't stand the atmosphere when we are worshiping. Then, the next time I saw him we had the same discussion, with the same result; and again, a third time he led us into the same discussion, which was going to end in the same place as before. I had to stop the conversation and say, "Do you really want to have this conversation again? We will just get to the same place. "

There seems to be some kind of evil blockage that the enemy uses to keep us from understanding what is affecting us, and the only way we can understand is to be delivered of it by Jesus. Only when it is gone can we realize how terribly we had been affected. Once we start getting deliverance, we suddenly realize how evil was affecting us all along.

This stuff is tricky; evil wants us to think that it is ourselves who originate our thoughts and behaviors. It wants us to think, "This is just how I am; this is just me. " But that might not be who you are; it might well be evil just messing with you. Some mindset that could have been there from birth is so very familiar, but when it is gone, you realize that it wasn't really who you are at all. If you don't believe this, just go to the Lord humbly and ask Him to set you free of any blockages in your mind. He is perfectly capable of opening your mind to revelation and understanding about what is happening.

Keep in mind that any lack of understanding might not be caused by a demon but could be an evil cultural mindset that needs to be broken or removed, one which originates from the demonic influences that are all around us. Additionally, even though we generally operate in a Christian culture within the church, there seems to be an evil mindset that has been planted down through the generations to keep believers bound. It is not just in the United States or in Africa; it affects Christians globally. If evil can't steal your salvation, it seems the next best thing it can do is to deceive Christians so they don't become free, powerful and victorious in Christ.

CHAPTER 20
WHY PEOPLE WON'T RECEIVE PRAYER

There is a burden on my heart for the members of the global Church, not just the congregation or denomination where I usually worship. I know that through prayer ministry many could be healed and delivered, but because most members of the global Christian Church haven't been fully taught, they don't understand. Many believe that healing is for others and have little or no faith that God cares enough to heal them personally. They believe in healing through prayer, but they think that it is so rare that the odds are against their ever receiving it. Or, they may have a mistaken belief that healing will only come through famous ministers. These sad misconceptions prevent many people from requesting prayer ministry.

The burden I feel is a compassion that the Lord has put within me. That compassion has been good because it has caused me to ask various men of God for reasons people don't accept prayer. I asked Pastor Albie Pearson, who has a powerful healing and deliverance ministry, "Why won't people come for their prayer and healing?" His answer was one word, "Pride". He then quoted 1 Peter 5:5-7:

Likewise you younger people, submit yourselves to your elders. Yes, all of you be submissive to one another, and be clothed with humility, for "God resists the proud, but gives grace to the humble. "*Therefore humble yourselves under the mighty hand of God, that He may exalt you in due time, casting all your care upon Him, for He cares for you.*

I really connected with the sentence, *Therefore humble yourselves under the mighty hand of God, that He may exalt you in due time.*

Again, why don't people come for prayer? They would have to humble themselves, and pride seems to block the act of humility. But look at the last part of the verse, ...*that He may exalt you in due time.* We all want to be exalted, don't we? Doesn't that sound good? The apostle Peter wrote that humility under the mighty hand of God was necessary first, and sometimes when I am ministering, I can see the hand of God come down. When that occurs. I know for sure that something good is happening!

> *Therefore humble yourselves under the mighty hand of God, that He may exalt you in due time.*
>
> — I PETER 5:6

Albie also told me of a time when he was ministering in the Lord's power and many miracles were happening. Several people had been healed of cancer, but then the miracles stopped. He inquired of the Lord and heard, "You are ministering without My love. " Albie changed his ministry style from moving in his flesh to operating out of the love of God for the people, and the miracles returned.

In conversation with Dr. Paul Cox, I explained what was going on in my heart regarding my sadness for the people of the church. I asked, "Why don't the people come for prayer?" His reply was, "The church loves to talk about God, but they don't want to engage with Him!" When he said that, I got an immediate 'hit' from the Lord confirming that Paul was speaking the truth.

I also called Dr. Tom Griner to explain what was going on in my heart and asked the same question, "Why don't the people come for prayer?" He answered, "They don't come because it is too costly. They would have to open up, humble themselves, and let go. " His words reminded me of someone whom I invited to come for prayer, and she said that she didn't want to come because she cries easily and would wind up crying. I thought to myself, "So what if you cry? Many people do, but the healing is so worth it. " I believe that Tom is correct; there is a cost. You might have to feel remorse, or worse yet, the pain of things that happened in the past. The logic sometimes seems to be, "If I come for prayer I will have to feel, and that might not be comfortable so I will just not do it. "

Watching a video on YouTube of a teaching by Prophet Michael Dalton of Desert Christian Community Church from January 3, 2018, I finally heard an answer to my question:

Most prophetic people, because they discern the heart of people, get agitated easily; because they can see and discern that people are not responding to the will of God, they take it personally because they recognize that if you would just obey God, God would bless you. So, when prophets, prophetic people, worshipers, teachers, ministers; whenever they see people not going for it, they get offended internally. I hope this is helping people. So, what you have to do instead of getting offended, you have to go into intercession. You have to pray for the ones whom God has sent you to minister to or you will get offended; and the moment you get offended, you shut down your own ministry. Because God will not let you minister to those you don't love. The moment you get offended at people, God also causes the level of grace you carry to begin to diminish because you cannot move in grace and judgment. I had someone say to me once, "I have never seen a nice prophet. " I had preached at their church and prophesied all night and they said, "You are the first nice prophet I have met. " They said all the rest of them seem so upset. So many times, people go around expecting that to be the reality, but the truth of that is (now hear me when I say it) their gift might be mature, but their soul is not. You can have a mature gift and an immature soul. You have a lot of people that have matured in their gift, but they did not work on their character. And if you mature your character you never get angry with the people you were sent to help. Because you remember that you also are they.

When I heard this, I knew that it was a word from the Lord for me. It really helped me understand what I was going through. The Lord continues to show me what He can do for people; and I need to just stay in a place of love, interceding in prayer, and trusting that the Lord in His time will bring a person or people into a place of healing and deliverance. Before the Lord taught me, along with teaching from my friends and teachers, I didn't believe or understand. As Michael Dalton says, "I also are they. "

Let us continue to pray and intercede for those in need of healing and deliverance as the Lord highlights them to us though His wonderful Spirit. Let's ask Him to bring them to a place where they will reach out for help; just a text message, a phone call or a few minutes on the Internet can connect people to someone who can help them. Then through prayer, lives and even generations can be changed into a beautiful bride for Christ.

CHAPTER 21

THE FLESH OR A DEMON?

There is a key question for Christians looking for freedom: Is my behavior or are my thoughts caused by my flesh or by a demon? When I examine my thoughts or actions, I often ask myself that question because one of these two reasons is at the root of our sin. In Romans 6:6, Paul referred to our flesh as 'our old man':

...knowing this, that our old man was crucified with Him, that the body of sin might be done away with, that we should no longer be slaves of sin.

So how do we know what is behind our behavior? My advice is to ask the Lord. He knows what is going on inside and can reveal it to you. It may be helpful to remember that demons compel. If a sinful behavior feels like a compulsion, it is quite suspect that the demonic is behind it. I could have listed a thousand things that demons compel people do to but have mentioned and illustrated only a few to help you understand what behaviors the demonic can produce. The unfortunate truth is that they are messing with both secular people and Christians, many who remain clueless. Many Christians believe that demons can have influence on them and that the demons are floating around and affecting them somehow. They are correct in understanding that demons can and do move around in the atmosphere, with regional spirits affecting large geographical areas and thus affecting Christians too. However, the spirit world is much more complicated than this simplistic view. Evil spirits (demons) not only inhabit Christians but there can also be many of them. During ministry we discovered demons that are both in and out at the same time. We have run across a demon spirit that looks like an octopus that attaches on the back of the neck of the person while connecting to the spinal cord inside with its beak; it is on the outside and the inside at the same time. One person we ministered to had this unclean spirit on his neck for so many years that he had suffered damage to his cervical disc. Several years before we prayed for him, he had surgery on his neck to repair the disk, and now that the Lord has removed it, his neck is doing much better.

Another spirit that we have found is on the outside but is connected down the side of a person (usually the left, but occasionally on the right); it's name is Doppelganger and is half inside and half outside of the person it is attached to. We have seen it move behind the person trying to hide from us. It causes rebellion, double minded-ness and makes people want to do the opposite of what others want to do. So if someone says, "Let's go right," the person with the Doppel-ganger spirit wants to go left.

I once asked Pastor Albie Pearson if the demons are inside or outside a person? He answered, "Inside or outside, I don't care. They have to go!" I love the simplicity and truth of his answer.

After you receive some deliverance, either by commanding them to come out of yourself or by allowing someone to cast them out, you will feel the release and a sense of peace, accompanied by new or different behaviors. For example, if the demon that causes rage is gone, then you will notice that you no longer are raging at other people. As you begin to understand that the behavior was not yourself, your flesh, you will begin to be on the lookout for other behaviors that could be from demons. I use 'flesh' to describe the part of us that was corrupted in the fall of mankind and am not only talking about the physical body but also about the corrupt nature we received or inherited in the womb. 'Carnal' is another word to describe the flesh, as is our 'sinful nature'.

It is a misunderstanding to believe that after one prayer session all demons have left, and when I hear a deliverance minister tell someone that they are free after just one session I cringe. That implies that they are completely free, but how could any minister know that for sure? I am saddened by the declaration of such a misconception; it would be more correct to say, "I believe that you have received some deliverance," and then encourage them to observe what happens over time. In my experience, it can take many sessions to pray off evil, layer upon layer; usually there are many demonic rights. Since I realized that all Christians can have demons occupying them and have begun to receive prayer myself, I can identify over twenty that have left me. I share this because I believe I am not that much different than others in the church. Some demons were generational and some I picked up because of sinful behavior. Agreeing with gossip or speaking it can open one up to demonization. Even over recent years I have had some enter me, realized their presence, and was able to self-deliver through prayer. When that didn't work, I had someone with authority pray for me and I was delivered.

> "We must pray like we're using a sniper rifle, not a shotgun."
>
> — DR. PAUL C. COX

The correct spiritual diagnosis is essential for us to overcome because in order to know how to pray for others or ourselves, we need know what we are up against. In prayer ministry, I have found that the most specific prayer gets the best results. Dr. Paul Cox says, "We must pray like we're using a sniper rifle, not a shotgun." In other words, our prayers are most effective when carefully targeted toward the evil in our scopes.

Remember Paul's words in Romans 6:6? *Our old man was crucified with Him.* If we want to overcome the flesh, the answer is to crucify it, because the Lord canceled the claims that sin has on our flesh. Galatians 5:24 lends more insight:

And those who are Christ's have crucified the flesh with its passions and desires.

We cannot cast out the flesh; to overcome it we must crucify it; we must die to our evil passions and desires. If we have a problem with gossip and slander after the evil spirit is cast out of us, then we must take each thought captive before we say it, and if it is gossip or slander, we must choose silence. This is crucifying the flesh.

We are not, however, able to crucify a demon; those need to be cast out and we do that in the authority that God has given us:

And these signs will follow those who believe: In My name they will cast out demons; they will speak with new tongues; they will take up serpents; and if they drink anything deadly, it will by no means hurt them; they will lay hands on the sick, and they will recover. (Mark 16:17-18)

CHAPTER 22
'GETTING ONTO IT'

After some deliverance, many times you may experience a certain behavior, and wonder if a demon is causing it. One example that is always suspected is an obsessive thought about someone or something. Another example is feeling a lack of peace. Many times, I have had demons in or on me and, sure enough, after some prayer the behavior was gone. I call this, "Getting onto it," because once you are onto it, the root of the behavior is revealed, and you know that with deliverance prayer it will soon be gone.

'Mary's' Story:

A woman we'll call Mary, who has been a Christian for many years, asked my wife and me to meet with her for some prayer time. During the ministry session, Mary explained that she had been on anti-depressants for a few years and had decided to reduce the dose to see how her behavior would be with a lower dose. Slowly, over a period of months, she had reduced the medication and had begun to notice that when her friends became grandparents, she felt jealous. She thought, "Why should I be jealous? I should be rejoicing with them. " As Mary examined her thoughts, she began to wonder if there was a demon affecting them; she didn't just write it off as her flesh. She decided to spend some time with us to see if there would be healing.

During the prayer session, I bound the demon of jealousy and told it to leave in the name of Jesus. Immediately, Mary said, "Oh wow! I feel something happening in my head. " I thought to myself, "Oh, this is good; Jesus is doing something. " Mary then began to bend forward and to breathe heavily, with deep breaths in and out. This was a form of manifesting, which seemed fine to me because I knew a demon was leaving. But then Mary said, "It is choking me! I can't breathe. " Anne laid her hand on Mary's throat and began to pray. I commanded the demon to loose her throat, and it immediately did. Mary continued to manifest with the deep breathing for a few minutes, and then it was done. When I asked her what it felt like, she said that something was happening in her head. She explained that it felt like there was string wrapped around and around in her mind, and that Jesus was pulling one end of the string and it was unwrapping outward. I called Mary a couple of days later to see how she was doing, and she said that she felt great and the only way she could describe it was that she felt delivered! Mary was watching her behavior, and she was looking for healing. Mary 'got onto it' and decided to get prayer. The blood of Jesus is sufficient; Jesus is our deliverer, and when we ask for freedom, He is always ready to respond.

Critical Spirit:

A close friend stopped by our house one morning so we could grade some coffee. (We both are in the coffee business and like to keep our tasting skills calibrated so it is fun to discuss quality and flavors of new coffees that we have roasted.) Anne was in the living room with us when I began to tell a story to my friend, but she interrupted and began to tell the story her way. Because this is a long-time close friend, I felt safe to stop Anne and to say in a polite voice, "Please don't interrupt and take over my stories. " She replied that I wasn't giving enough detail about the story, so she was going finish it. After my friend left, she let me know that she was quite upset that I would correct her in front of another person. I had thought it was OK because this was a close friend, but then I wondered, "Why do I correct her only in front of close friends? Could there be an unclean spirit operating in me?" I asked the Lord if it was a spirit causing me to act that way and the word 'critical' came to mind. I asked the Lord if I have a critical spirit and got a hit. I went into the back room and tried to cast it out of myself but felt no deliverance. A few days later I called one of my deliverance friends and explained that I believed I had a critical sprit and asked for her to pray for me. She said that she had dealt with a critical spirit before in a man. Because he was extremely critical, she didn't recognize criticism in me, and so she didn't believe I could have a critical spirit. I said that I can be quite critical, and that one of my employees had quit because of it. That convinced her to pray for me and tell the critical spirit in me to leave. Before she even finished the prayer, I discerned (felt) it go. Over the next few days, I felt a subtle, but noticeable, change in my thoughts and personality. I 'got onto' another unclean spirit and now it is gone.

Spirit of Stupor:

Another spirit that had plagued me was a spirit of stupor. I had noticed that while ministering with Anna, I would get tired and want to go home to take a nap. Knowing that deliverance can make you tired, I assumed that was the reason. I also noticed that when I was at an Aslan's Place meeting, I could not stay awake: I would nod off, even if I'd slept nine hours and had several cups of coffee. Over the years it kept getting worse, to the point that I said to myself, "What is it with me while I am in the ministry room?"

I was doing a deliverance session with Anna and had a cup of coffee before the session so I would be awake and alert, but still began to nod off. After the session, I 'got onto it' and began to discuss the issue with Anna. She said it was a spirit of stupor, also known as a spirit of slumber; she then prayed for me and I discerned the spirit leave.

That same night, though I could not believe how tired I had been during the session, I stayed up watching television until midnight. The next morning, I woke up feeling quite different from the norm. Instead of getting up feeling very groggy and needing a cup of coffee and taking half an hour to become alert, I was wide-awake when I first awakened. I went to work with a new zeal, much more alert than normal, and found myself thinking quickly with a new desire to get things done. The spirit of stupor had been affecting me much more than just trying to make me nod off in school and during prayer sessions; it had compromised my whole day. I have no idea how I picked that spirit up, but I do know that it had been getting stronger over four years. I am quite pleased that spirit is gone and is now wandering in the dry places.

A spirit of stupor isn't something I named; it's biblical:

Just as it is written: "God has given them a spirit of stupor, Eyes that they should not see And ears that they should not hear, To this very day." (Romans 11:8)

Strong's concordance defines stupor as:[1]

katanuxis: stupefaction
Original Word: κατάνυξις, εως, ἡ
Part of Speech: Noun, Feminine
Transliteration: *katanuxis*
Phonetic Spelling: (kat-an'-oox-is)
Definition: stupefaction
Usage: deep sleep, torpor, insensibility, stupor.

My Prayer:

Thank You, Lord, for being my deliverer. Thank You for exercising loving-kindness, judgment and righteousness throughout all the earth.

CHAPTER 23
TIPS FOR DELIVERANCE MINISTRY

To really understand how deliverance works and how to discern what is happening both before and after deliverance, I believe that one must first experience it. How good a minister can you be if you haven't experienced what it is like? That is one of the ways we learn, and once you have had some deliverance prayer, the Lord might put a burden on your heart to help others.

 The Lord planted a desire in me to help others become free.

— JOSEF ROUSEK

That is what happened to me; the Lord planted a desire in me to help others become free after I had a few deliverance sessions. It worked out great because I was able to study under several very gifted teachers, and all of them had prayed for me before I began to study under them. I highly recommend finding someone who has been doing deliverance ministry for quite a while and asking if they will pray for you. If they are gifted, anointed, and the kind of person you would like to spend time under their teaching, you could ask to sit in on some of their sessions as a learning experience.

When doing prayer ministry, I am careful only to minister to men one on one. If there is a session with a woman, my wife or a female friend will always be present. If no woman is available to attend the session, it is rescheduled. We must remember that many times people who come in for prayer are wounded and under the control of evil. Who is the accuser of the brothers? Satan, of course, and his minions of false accusation, gossip, etc. would love to spread some rumors around. It is a setup to destroy a reputation if one ministers directly to a member of the opposite sex. When you minister with a partner or observer, a recipient will have trouble making false accusations of inappropriate behavior.

For a short time, we invited people to our home for prayer. Then one Saturday my children were home when a woman my wife and I were praying for began manifesting, screaming extremely loud and long and with a piercing high pitch. Our children, in their teens at that time, were in their bedrooms. When they put on winter clothing and walked out through the living room door, I decided to pray somewhere else in the future. If available, a church would be ideal: a safe and neutral setting maintains privacy for you and your family. Having someone that you have ministered to in the past ringing your doorbell asking for prayer for a panic attack is not my idea of good family time!

It can be helpful to ask people in advance why they want prayer. I ask what is going on so I can begin to intercede for them. Many times, the Lord will show me how to pray before I arrive at the session.

When someone requests prayer, evil hears the conversation, which often starts a spiritual war. It is common for people to call back and cancel; evil has made them afraid to show up or has convinced them that it is not really evil that is the problem; it is just the self and they should be able to handle it. They might even feel that the problem no longer exists. It seems the longer they wait before the appointment, the more likely they will change their mind and cancel. The Bible says that the devil comes to lie, steal and destroy. He can steal their freedom and keep them stuck in his evil web by trying to prevent ministry; but if the person wants prayer badly enough, their self-will can prevail.

When a person shows up for prayer, I invite them into the room and visit with them for a short time. I always have some tissues available, a couple of Aslan's prayer manuals, a Bible, a notebook, and a laptop computer. As written previously, I highly value the ministry of Dr. Paul Cox at Aslan's Place, so much so that his generational prayer model will be provided later.

Giving advice and teaching:

During a deliverance session, time should be managed. People that have come for prayer for the first time may be nervous and want to talk a lot. When you ask why they want prayer, they may ramble on and on. The prayer minister must lead the session in order to have an effective ministry time. Remember it is a deliverance session, not a counseling session. Some crosstalk is necessary to help understand how to pray, but it must be managed to leave time for prayer.

It is both polite and considerate to do some cross-talking during the session. At times, I can understand that the problem they are seeking help for is not just about deliverance but also about understanding situations and people. Other times, after listening to the Lord about how to pray, I will switch from a time of deliverance to a time of giving advice or teaching. I am not a trained counselor, so I do not use the word 'counsel'. There are biblical concepts that can help people to function better in life that may need to be taught, and encouragement can also be healing, so feel free to lift up someone in those ways. It is always good to say how brave someone is to have come in and to have shared such intimate details of their life. Praising them for making the appointment, showing up and seeking freedom and healing is helpful.

Praying for Couples:

Praying with couples can be quite rewarding. Sometimes the spouse just wants to be there for emotional support and not for prayer. Other times both are looking for prayer, so I just listen to the Lord and go with His direction regarding which person to pray for first. One way to minister to a couple is to meet with both to get an understanding for the dynamics of the relationship, bring them in separately for prayer, and finally bring them in together.

One method for couples that I like is to ask them to sit in chairs or stand facing each other, hold each other's hands and look into each other eyes. I then ask to them repeat after me and then speak healing sentences that are to be spoken to each other. For example, "Cindy, please forgive me for yelling at you. I am ashamed for how I acted. Will you forgive me?" Or, "I am sorry for putting my job in front of my family. I was hiding out at work from our family. Lord Jesus, help me to change my behavior. I value You and love You. Will you forgive me?"

Speaking it out sincerely while looking into the eyes of a spouse is quite powerful and can bring effective healing, and such an action aligns with biblical principles:

> A wholesome tongue is a tree of life, But perverseness in it breaks the spirit. (Proverbs 15:4)

> Death and life are in the power of the tongue, and those who love it will eat its fruit. (Proverbs 18:21)

Death and life are in the power of the tongue, which means there is life-giving power in spoken words. When we have been hurt, an apology can bring life that facilitates healing. Often, having been wounded by another's words, we are longing for that person to ask for forgiveness. We must not forget that the tongue is a tree of life, and speaking truth is a powerful way to establish healing.

If the couple is married, sometimes I lead them in a short wedding ceremony at the end of the last session, asking the Lord to reunite them. I have them repeat wedding vows and then declare that they are now husband and wife. If they want to kiss, so much the better. Marriage was created by God, and a powerful spiritual re-unification ceremony can tie people back together in a refreshed and renewed relationship.

Praying for healing:

In order to get the best results, we must pray accurately. If the problem is caused by an evil spirit, we must cast it out; if it is a generational right, we ask Jesus to break it. But if it is neither of these problems, then we will need to pray for healing.

We ministered to a woman with Meniere's disease, which is an inner ear disease that is caused by a bacterial infection that causes a lack of balance. In this case, the woman's affliction was so bad that she would lose her balance and fall down; it could happen in the house, the bank or the supermarket. Often she would be hurt from the fall, causing other painful injuries. She had been on medication for twenty years, but the condition had not only continued but had become worse. I didn't know if we would be doing deliverance or healing when we came together for the prayer session. My ministry partner had done some homework before we showed up for the appointment. It turned out that Meniere's requires healing payer, so after some time of talking, I laid my hands on the woman's head and we all asked God to heal her. My hands got quite warm, which is always a good sign, but we couldn't tell if God had healed her so we went home knowing that in time we would find out. The woman believed that she was healed and decided to stop taking her medication for the first time in twenty years (note: we do not recommend this before consulting with a doctor). Over the next few days, her lack of balance subsided, and she had no symptoms. Through prayer, she had been healed and she has had not had any problems since. It is not really that rare to see someone get healed; I have seen it happen many times, and after all, the Bible says that some have gifts of healing:

And Jesus went about all Galilee, teaching in their synagogues, preaching the gospel of the kingdom, and healing all kinds of sickness and all kinds of disease among the people. (Matthew 4:23)

Most assuredly, I say to you, he who believes in Me, the works that I do he will do also; and greater works than these he will do, because I go to My Father. (John 14:12)

...to another faith by the same Spirit, to another gifts of healings by the same Spirit... (1 Corinthians 12:9)

Don't be afraid to pray for healing; even if the person doesn't get healed, at least you tried in faith. I can assure you that if you don't try there won't be a healing. If you do try, you very easily could witness a miracle because God is perfectly able to heal, not just once but many times. He is just waiting for someone to ask. Remember, you don't need much faith, only as much as a mustard seed and that isn't very big. Just pray and believe that God can heal, and many times He will.

The key is in your mouth:

The key to our freedom is in our mouth. With the mouth we can sin, but also with the mouth we can also repent; with the mouth we can curse but with the same mouth we can ask the Lord to break the curse. The mouth can produce words that torment someone, and it can be used to lead someone out of torment. The mouth does so much more than vibrate the air to cause sound waves, and what a powerful spiritual tool it is!

For by your words you will be justified, and by your words you will be condemned. " (Matthew 12:37)

Yes, by our words we will be justified and by our words we will be condemned. Have you ever taken the time to realize what this scripture is really saying? Easton's 1897 Bible Dictionary defines justification as:

> ...a forensic term opposed to condemnation. As regards its nature, it is the judicial act of God, by which he pardons all the sins of those who believe in Christ, and accounts, accepts, and treats them as righteous in the eye of the law, i. e. , as conformed to all its demands. In addition to the pardon (q. v.) of sin, justification declares that all the claims of the law are satisfied in respect of the justified. It is the act of a judge and

not of a sovereign. The law is not relaxed or set aside, but is declared to be fulfilled in the strictest sense; and so the person justified is declared to be entitled to all the advantages and rewards arising from perfect obedience to the law (Rom. 5:1-10).

None of us, no matter how hard we try, can live a sinless life. But by our words we will be declared to be entitled to all the advantages and rewards arising from the perfect obedience to the law.

> ...that if you confess with your mouth the Lord Jesus and believe in your heart that God has raised Him from the dead, you will be saved. For with the heart one believes unto righteousness, and with the mouth confession is made unto salvation. (Romans 10:9-10)

Again, *for with the mouth confession is made unto salvation.* The mouth brings us into salvation; the mouth also brings us into our deliverance; the key is truly in our mouth:

> If we confess our sins, He is faithful and just to forgive us our sins and to cleanse us from all unrighteousness. (1 John 1:9)

> Confess your trespasses to one another, and pray for one another, that you may be healed. The effective, fervent prayer of a righteous man avails much. (James 5:16)

In both of the above scriptures, the word 'confess' implies that our sins or trespasses are to be spoken by the mouth to another. This is an important biblical teaching that must be understood by the prayer minister as well as the person requesting prayer. In James 5:16, the confession leads to healing of the person, and this is exactly what we are looking for isn't it? It is important to look for the confession before the effective fervent prayer begins.

CHAPTER 24
COMMON DEMONIC BEHAVIORS

When you are casting out demons, don't close your eyes. For your safety and to help you understand what is going on, always keep them open. Then, if the person starts to manifest you can keep them safe, and also protect yourself. When people manifest, a demon takes control of their body and can cause them injury. For example, you really don't want them to fall onto a glass coffee table.

Watch the eyes of the person being prayed for because demons often leave through the eyes. You will see a distinct blink, or several blinks, as they leave. When demons come forward to take control of someone during prayer, they can look out their eyes; sometimes the eyes will change from the natural color to a dark black that emanates evil hatred. The first time I saw this happen, it really creeped me out, and I said to the demon, "You are not scaring me away. It is you that is leaving. " Several did come out of the woman, and she was healed of epilepsy.

Stay alert when casting out demons. Demons can speak from a woman with the voice of a man and conversely, men can speak with the voice of a woman. Demons can change facial expressions too; once I watched as the face of a beautiful woman in her forties changed into the face of an old witch. I must admit, that was quite spooky; but I was ministering with someone else and we just kept on praying.

Demons can also exit via the mouth. You may notice yawning, or burping, and often the client will say, "Oh wow, it is leaving out my mouth. "

In fact, demons can exit through any orifice in the body. Sometimes they leave as flatulence. Once as I cast a demon out of a man after church, he got a funny look on his face while I was praying. I asked how he felt, and he said he urgently needed to go outside to pass gas. He hurried out to the parking lot to pass the demon out through his rectum.

Demons can also leave the body where there is not an orifice. One exited via my own body just below the sternum while I was lying in a recliner, reading a book by Dr. Paul Cox. I had a thought that I might have a spirit that he was talking about and decided to try self-deliverance. I named the evil spirit and told it to come out. My body began to tighten up and go stiff and I thought to myself, "Wow this is very cool, I am manifesting!" I could feel the evil spirit leave my body out my upper abdomen, and after a few seconds the manifestation stopped, and I felt my muscles relax. I was quite excited because I had seen hundreds of people manifest demons during ministry and always wondered what it felt like. I was so excited that I had both self-delivered and manifested, so I immediately called Tom Griner and excitedly said, "Tom I just did self-deliverance and I manifested when the demon came out of me!" There was dead silence on the other end of the phone line. I think Tom didn't know what to think of me. You have to admit that is an odd phone call!

If you ask demons questions they can answer in English or sometimes they start speaking in a demonic tongue. I don't like the sound of the evil tongue, so when they start speaking it, I bind them and tell them to be quiet. That usually works, but not always. Sometimes I just have to listen to it until the right for it to be there can be determined. I prayed for one person for over several days, and in each session, she would manifest as soon as I walked into the room. Obviously, I wasn't leading the person in a correct prayer to break the legal right the demons had to stay in her, and/or I didn't have enough authority for my prayers to blast them out. Finally, at the beginning of the next ministry session I decided to ask the demon what right he had to be in the woman. I causally said, "What right do you have to be in this child of the most high God?" The answer I got surprised me. An evil man's voice came out of the woman in a loud screaming wail and said, "I have a right!" Later the demon told me it was a boar. My friend said to it, "No you are just a pig," but we used the information to lead us to a prayer in the Aslan's Place prayer manual that mentions Bacco, the boar. After she read the prayer and identified with the sin of her ancestors of worshiping the pagan god, Bacco the boar, its right to stay in her was broken and we were able to cast it out. I don't recommend talking to demons, but in this case, it helped show us the way to pray effectively which led to a wonderful deliverance. Mark 5:8-13(NKJV) says:

> For He said to him, "Come out of the man, unclean spirit!" Then He asked him, "What is your name?" And he answered, saying, "My name is Legion; for we are many."Also he begged Him earnestly that He would not send them out of the country. Now a large herd of swine was feeding there near the mountains. So all the demons begged Him, saying, "Send us to the swine, that we may enter them." And at once Jesus gave them permission. Then the unclean spirits went out and entered the swine (there were about two thousand); and the herd ran violently down the steep place into the sea, and drowned in the sea.

Here we learn that it is not forbidden for us to speak to demons through the example of Jesus. However, while it is acceptable biblically, it is best to avoid it because demons are liars, and I prefer to spend my time listing to the Lord's truth.

It is common for an African prayer minister to ask the demon his or her name so they can address it by name when commanding it to come out. They believe it is worthwhile to get the name, and I don't object. I know that the more specific I pray, the better the results I get but I prefer to get the name of the evil spirit through prophetic discernment rather than opening a dialog with the demon. Once such a discussion is begun, it's not always easy to get the demon to shut up.

Sometimes I don't hear the demon's names prophetically, so I have learned another way to pray, which is identifying it by the behavior it causes. For example, if the person is cutting themselves, whether you know it because they have told you or you can see scarring on their arms, you can pray, "All unclean spirits that cause (person's name) to cut himself, I bind you; self-hate, I bind you. Leave now and go to the feet of Jesus. "If I only say, "All unclean spirits that cause this person to cut himself," I am using a blanket prayer that doesn't name each unclean spirit. It can be quite an effective prayer anyway, but it's better to be as specific as possible. If I add "self hate" to the prayer I am getting more specific. Remember that there are many spirits causing sinful behavior, so don't hesitate to command all of them causing the behavior to leave.

The behavior of people manifesting demons can be quite varied. A man that had come to our home group for the first time stopped us during our group prayer and requested prayer. He said there was opposition coming against him, and I knew from that description and the tone of his voice that he was under demonic attack; he was mildly manifesting. Our home group is quite a mature group of Christians who all love to pray for deliverance, so we bound it, cast it out and the man left the meeting with more freedom. This type of light manifestation is common, and the resolution for this man is what I consider an excellent Christian meeting. Someone comes bound and leaves freer.

Other times a person manifesting can be quite dramatic. It is common for them to fall down and to thrash around, sometimes screaming very loudly, growling or moaning. The demons can cause a person to hurt themselves on furniture or other surroundings. That is why it is best to learn how to minister in such a way that people don't manifest, because who wants to wrestle with someone in your church or house? If you break the generational right that the evil has to be in the person with generational deliverance prayers before you begin to cast out the demons, severe manifestations are rare

During outdoor evangelistic meetings in Africa, I have seen demons cause people to take off running at full speed away from the presence of God. People manifesting usually can't walk but sometimes if you get them up off the ground with one person holding each arm you can help them move, but often they have to be carried. Demons can cause people to spin like a top, to slither like a snake, to get combative, or to move around like a staggering drunk.

When we minister in the deliverance tent in Africa, we see all kinds of bizarre behavior. Sometimes demons will cause people to charge the door trying to get out, so we usually station a man at the door to keep the people who are manifesting inside the tent. At the Victoria Falls, Zimbabwe meeting, a very strong woman was manifesting; we had been praying for her and the demon made a last-ditch effort to get out of the tent. She got into a linebacker stance and took off running full speed with her head down. I saw what was happing and was able to jump out of the way as the woman ran headfirst into the tent wall, trying to break out. Luckily, the tent was set up strongly and she just bounced back. At the very moment of impact the demon left, and when she bounced back, she got up in her right mind.

Several times I have seen a seen a demon that had apparently been in a male professional prize fighter but had left the fighter either through deliverance or after he died and gone into a woman. She would bob, bounce and throw punches just like a professional boxer. I really don't want to get my jaw broken in a deliverance tent, so I am always quite alert while ministering there.

Fortunately, the above examples are deliverance tent stories that generally do not apply during prayer ministry sessions. If you are praying for someone that manifests, don't get too upset about it; just try to keep the person safe, and let God do the deliverance. I continue to pray for the person, but don't repeatedly tell the demon to come out because it can take an hour or more for the evil spirit to completely leave the person and give them back control of their body and mind. Just let the deliverance progress, believing that the evil spirit is being driven out by the Holy Spirit. Once the demon has left, ask them how they feel and lead them in a prayer asking the Holy Spirit to come in and to fill their mind and body.

Sometimes it will look like the person is delivered but what has happened is the demon has gone back into the mind and will give back the control of their body but doesn't completely leave. If that happens, pray some more to see if you get more results. If not, reschedule a prayer session believing that God will show you how to minister more accurately next time. You might want to contact a prayer minister with more experience and authority to attend that session.

CHAPTER 25
GENERATIONAL CURSES

If you want to help people get free, it is important to look at the biblical teaching regarding generational curses. This is a subject rarely understood, and in turn rarely taught from the pulpit. But Dr. Paul Cox provides a great teaching in his book, *Come up Higher*, which is reiterated here with his permission. [1]

https://www.amazon.com/dp/0983454671

I have noticed that many do not understand the actual biblical meaning of the word curse. The English word curse had broad connotations, ranging from a simple synonym for misfortune to a condition of unrelieved hopelessness brought on by supernatural forces, magical or divine. Therefore, when we read the translated Old Testament and see the English word curse, we assume that we understand the meaning of that word. However, in reality the four Hebrew words that are translated 'a curse' have many more than four different meanings.

My serendipity about the word curse began when I noticed that many books about the nature of curses listed as a primary source an article in the *Journal of Biblical Literature* entitled, *The Problem of "Curse" in the Hebrew Bible*. This doctoral dissertation by H. C. Brichto includes a multi-language study of the word curse and clearly delineates the precise meaning of each of the four Hebrew words translated as curse in the Old Testament.

Brichto makes it clear that the starting point for our understanding of the word curse, by definition, is an imprecation. An imprecation is an exact formula of a series of words by which a curse is invoked. Therefore, to say that some evil took place in the family line that cursed or brought a curse on subsequent generations would be a misuse of the word curse. The word curse is a formulized set of words uttered against someone else. So, what are these Hebrew words?

According to Brichto, four Hebrew words are translated into the English as curse: *alah, arur, qualet,* and *qabab*. Only *qabab* means imprecation. Here is the explanation of the other words:

1. *Alah*—The number one meaning is "oath. "An oath is a promise with the understanding that a penalty will take place (curse) if there is a false assertion of railing of one to keep his word. Although other scholars have translated alah as an imprecation, Brichto's argument for the definition of alah is convincing.
2. *Arur*—The Version translates this word as "curse" sixty-two times, and as "bitterly" once; forms include to curse, cursed be he, to be cursed, cursed; to curse, lay under a curse, put a curse on, to be made a curse, be cursed. The word is best rendered "banned. " Its basic sense is best rendered "spell. "When applied to the earth or rain, it is a spell which bars fertility to men. When applied to men or animals, it bars them from the benefits of fertility or association with their fellow creatures. The power of the curse is derived from deity or an agency endowed by the god of the society with unusual powers.

3. *Qualet*—translated as "curse" thirty-nine times, "swifter" five times, "light thing" five times, "vile" four times, "lighter" four times, "despise" three times, "abated" twice, "ease" twice, "light" twice, "lighten" twice, "slightly" twice, and is translated miscellaneously twelve times. The word actually means to be slight, be swift, be trifling, be of little account, be light, be abated (of water), to be swift, to be trifling, be of little account, to be swift, show oneself swift, to appear trifling, to be to trifling, be insignificant, to be lightly esteemed, to make despicable, to curse, to be cursed, to make light, lighten, to treat with contempt, bring contempt or dishonor, to shake, to whet, to shake oneself, to be moved to and fro. Qualet is best translated "abuse" or "to treat harshly or injuriously. "It is a general term for punishment, misfortune, disaster, or harm.

4. *Qabab, qabab*—A primitive root; eight occurrences; translates as "curse" seven times, and "at all" once. It means to curse, utter a curse against.

With this understanding, we can now carefully examine the passage in Deuteronomy 28:15-68. The Hebrew word translated as curse in the New King James Version in Deuteronomy 28:15 is *qualet*:

But it shall come to pass, if you do not obey the voice of the Lord your God, to observe carefully all His commandments and His statutes, which I command you today, that all these curses will come upon you and overtake you.

Rather than translating *qualet* as curse, a more accurate translation for *qualet* is misfortune, disaster, or harm. In other words, the evil that would come down the family line could result in generational misfortune, disaster, or harm.

Deuteronomy 28:20 uses another Hebrew word, *arur*:

The Lord will send on you cursing, confusion, and rebuke in all that you set your hand to do, until you are destroyed and until you perish quickly, because of the wickedness of your doings in which you have forsaken Me.

In this passage the Lord is saying that because of your sin, he will "ban" you from enjoying the benefits of his blessings.

An accurate reading of the Deuteronomy passage is that evil in a generational line will be passed down as an iniquity rather than a curse. The Old Testament word for iniquity is the Hebrew word *avah* meaning to bend or twist. The sin in a family line starts a twisting in that line, and that twisting is carried down through the line until it is broken by the power of the blood of Jesus Christ.

What happens when this generational iniquity is broken? The good news is that breaking this generational evil through the power of the blood of Jesus Christ releases the generational blessings giving to the family line. The word bless is a translation of the Hebrew word *barak* which means, "to endue with power for success, prosperity, fecundity, longevity." The generational iniquity covers up the blessings, which are available for thousands of generations.

As we can see from the above teaching the common term 'generational curse' that is so often used in the church would be more accurately described as 'generational iniquity', which gives evil 'generational spiritual legal rights' to affect the bloodline. Using the terminology 'generational curse' leads people to assume wrongly that God is doing some kind of incantation to the bloodline. Because the English language has only the one word 'curse' to describe four Hebrew words, the translation can be quite misleading. I prefer to use the term 'generational rights' to describe the effects of sin on the bloodline.

It really helps me to think of generational rights as iniquity (again, the Hebrew word *avah*, meaning to bend or twist). Because our genes are a double helix you can think of them as twisted. It is logical to me that the generational iniquity is carried down the generational line in the genes, and during generational deliverance, the genes are actually changed by God.

You might ask if the generational rights last for three to four generations then why do I pray for generations farther back than that? We can see that the below scriptures teach us that the iniquity of the fathers is visited upon the children and the children's children to the third and fourth generation:

Exodus 20:5 (NKJV): ...*you shall not bow down to them nor serve them. For I, the Lord your God, am a jealous God, visiting the iniquity of the fathers upon the children to the third and fourth generations of those who hate Me.*

Exodus 34:7 (NKJV): ...*keeping mercy for thousands, forgiving iniquity and transgression and sin, by no means clearing the guilty, visiting the iniquity of the fathers upon the children and the children's children to the third and the fourth generation.*

Numbers 14:18 (NKJV): *The Lord is long-suffering and abundant in mercy, forgiving iniquity and transgression; but He by no means clears the guilty, visiting the iniquity of the fathers on the children to the third and fourth generation.*

Jeremiah 32:18 (NKJV): *You show lovingkindness to thousands, and repay the iniquity of the fathers into the bosom of their children after them—the Great, the Mighty God, whose name is the Lord of hosts.*

If the curse is on a generational line, we can see in the natural or by the Spirit that it is affecting the generational line. We can understand its effects by talking to the person. We also know that the curses will not always affect each child in the next generation. It might skip some members or affect them all. The curse might even skip affecting an entire generation, but it has three to four generations to manifest the effects of itself. Let's use adultery as an example. If adultery is done by someone the sin might set up a generational curse. I say might, because "Nothing is always. " But if it does set up a curse, then it is very likely that several people in the next three to four generations will have the spirit of adultery that has gained access by the legal right of the curse. This evil spirit will drive them to commit adultery. Then the curse will be repowered for another three to four generations. This could go on for hundreds of generations. The only one who can break this curse is Jesus. So, for the generational line to get free of this curse, someone would have to become a Christian. But that alone may not be enough because specific prayer to identify and to break the source of the curse is generally needed. Yes, the Lord is sovereign and can break curses as he pleases without a person asking Him, but it doesn't usually happen that way. The person with the curse might have to identify with the sins of their forefathers. This is called identificational repentance. This is why I pray back to more than four generations. The generational iniquity could be repowering itself generation after generation.

Identificational repentance:

Identificational repentance happens when one identifies that his/her generational ancestors have sinned and fallen short of the right-eousness of God, and then that person confesses it before God. The concept is biblical, but it is rarely taught from the pulpit:

> *Then those of Israelite lineage separated themselves from all foreigners; and they stood and confessed their sins and the iniquities of their fathers.* (Nehemiah 9:2)

> *But if they confess their iniquity and the iniquity of their fathers, with their unfaithfulness in which they were unfaithful to Me, and that they also have walked contrary to Me.* (Leviticus 26:40)

In the above two scriptures, we can see examples of identificational repentance. Israelites are identifying with the sins and iniquity of their fathers and confessing their sins and the iniquities of their fathers. This concept is of key importance in generational deliverance. We are not able to ask the Lord for forgiveness for our fathers, but we are able to confess the sins of our fathers, therefore identifying before the Lord that they have sinned. We can then ask the Lord to break the consequences. This attitude of the heart pleases the Lord and there is much power in it. The Lord hears, has compassion, and removes the iniquities.

CHAPTER 26
REMOVING SPIRITUAL
ATTACHMENTS

When praying for deliverance, there are often evil spiritual attachments that are discerned and need to be removed for a person to gain freedom. These may include chains, snares on the ankles, black power cords that are plugged into the back, evil robes, evil headbands, and anything else that you can discern or see that is not from God. Many times, we can see darts stuck into someone's back, which are very likely to have been thrown by gossip and slander. There is power in your words that affects others far beyond what we realize, and this is a prime example. When I discern darts in someone's back, I simply grasp hold them with my hand, pull them out and drop them; I then discern with my hand if they are all gone. Recently we came across black wings on someone's back and when we walked behind him to remove them, the person jumped forward saying, "It doesn't like that!" After we asked the Lord to remove the wings, the person told us that he had been having a strong desire to get black wings tattooed on his chest.

At one crusade in Zambia, I ministered to a high school girl that had manifested and been carried into the deliverance tent by the ushers. The first night I prayed for her but couldn't discern any deliverance happening. She would kneel, sitting on her feet with her eyes rolled up so only the whites would show, and would weave back and forth like a snake, flicking her tongue out. It was obviously a snake demon, but it wouldn't leave even though I told it to. I left the tent and headed to the hotel for some rest. The next evening the same girl manifested during worship and was carried to the tent where I again spent some time praying for her, hoping the Holy Spirit would set her free. After some time, she came to her right mind and spoke to me a bit. I believed that the evil spirits had probably left, but the next night the same thing happened again; though frustrated, I continued to pray for her. No matter how much I commanded the snake demon to come out of her, it wouldn't. Her eyes again were rolling back so only the whites showed, and she was weaving and flicking out her tongue again. I finally had a thought about a wedding ring on her finger that was spiritual, because I couldn't see one in the natural, so I said, "Take the ring off!" After several commands for her to take it off, she slid the invisible ring off her wedding finger and laid it a couple feet in front of her. A few minutes later, she quickly reached out and grabbed the invisible ring and put it back on her left ring finger. I commanded her to take it off again and she did, so I kicked my foot where she had set it to move it across the tent floor so that she couldn't reach for it again. Then a Zambian prayer minister who was in the tent saw in the spirit that there were some strings around her wrists and ankles. We told her to take those off and after a while she did. The invisible ring, bracelets and anklets had been placed on her during a wedding ceremony when a powerful witchdoctor had decided to take her as his wife.

Once the evil jewelry had been removed, I instructed the snake to come out, but it still wouldn't leave. I told the snake that if it didn't come out, I would call down holy oil from heaven that would burn it badly, but it still didn't obey. I asked the Lord to pour His holy oil over the woman, after which her mouth opened wide and the large serpent started to come out. I commanded the girl to grab the snake with her hands and to pull it out of her mouth. Over and over she pulled the snake farther out, and when she was finished, she vomited something on the floor of the tent that looked like a broken raw egg. I was not seeing the egg in the Spirit but could actually see a physical egg in the natural! She stood up in her right mind and began to speak to me, so I led her in a prayer to receive the Lord but I could tell that she had prayed before and that she was a Christian. I asked her what that thing on the floor was that she had vomited, and she replied that the witch-doctor had given her that egg to eat when he had married her. I wondered how many months that egg had been in her stomach and why it hadn't been digested and realized that it must be some freaky thing from the spiritual realm that manifested in the natural realm. I asked the girl her name and told her when she sees the witchdoctor to run from him. She explained that that might be a problem because he was the principal of her high school. The witchdoctor was quite angry with me, so much so that he flew in the spirt realm a couple of months later to my house in the USA and came into my bedroom. When the Lord awoke me, I could see him floating down from above with his hands out, ready to choke me. I cried out the name of Jesus and he fled.

The reason I share this story is to illustrate the importance of removing all spiritual attachments so that the power of the evil will be broken. Until I did that, my prayers remained infective because the demons had legal rights to stay. Once the power of the invisible ring and strings was broken, I had enough authority to drive the snake demon out.

The African deliverance ministers tell me that sometimes bags of witchcraft (fetishes) that are still in the home also need to be burned before there is enough authority for deliverance to take place.

This story has a happy ending. My friend, Virtue, was this girl's friend. When I saw him a few years later I asked if he knew how she was doing. His reply was "She is doing wonderful! She is in my Bible study; she has a job and is quite happy. "

CHAPTER 27
SPIRITUAL AUTHORITY

Deliverance ministry is very complicated. Not only are there demons and curses, but also there are also many other evil factors that affect us. Fragments or pieces of our soul can become trapped in the dimensions; we can get stuck in Kronos (ungodly) time when we should be in Kairos (godly) time. Kronos is time in the manner of our clocks; the Greeks came up with it and we use it every day. Kairos time is God's time, which is where we need to be living. It is a good thing that we don't have to understand everything that is going on in the spiritual realms to begin to start praying for people because, again, deliverance does get complicated! We know that Jesus has given us authority and has commanded us to cast out demons, which is a good way to get started. Just use what you have and begin to pray for others believing that God is going to help the person.

Spiritual authority: what is it and how can we get it? Jesus has all authority in heaven and on earth, and He gives it to His people for the purpose of building each other up:

And Jesus came and spoke to them, saying, "All authority has been given to Me in heaven and on earth. (Matthew 28:18)

For even if I should boast somewhat more about our authority, which the Lord gave us for edification and not for your destruction, I shall not be ashamed. (2 Corinthians 10:8-10)

Therefore, I write these things being absent, lest being present I should use sharpness, according to the authority which the Lord has given me for edification and not for destruction. (2 Corinthians 13:10)

In Luke 9:1-2, we can see that Jesus gave His disciples power and authority over all demons and to cure diseases.

Then He called His twelve disciples together and gave them power and authority over all demons, and to cure diseases. He sent them to preach the kingdom of God and to heal the sick.

Jesus gives out power and authority to heal sicknesses, cast out demons, and trample on the enemy's attacks:

Then He appointed twelve, that they might be with Him and that He might send them out to preach, and to have power to heal sicknesses and to cast out demons. (Mark 3:14-15)

And He said to them, "I saw Satan fall like lightning from heaven. Behold, I give you the authority to trample on serpents and scorpions, and over all the power of the enemy, and nothing shall by any means hurt you. (Luke 10:18-19)

We've seen that power and authority go together (Luke 9:1-2, above), so if we are to have power over demons, we also need the authority given by Jesus. The disciples didn't have it until Jesus gave it to them. Then, though they had a lot of authority, it was not enough to cast out the deaf and dumb spirit in Mark 9:14-29:

And when He came to the disciples, He saw a great multitude around them, and scribes disputing with them. Immediately, when they saw Him, all the people were greatly amazed, and running to Him, greeted

*Him. And He asked the scribes, "What are you discussing with them?"
Then one of the crowd answered and said, "Teacher, I brought You my
son, who has a mute spirit. And wherever it seizes him, it throws him
down; he foams at the mouth, gnashes his teeth, and becomes rigid. So I
spoke to Your disciples, that they should cast it out, but they could not. "
He answered him and said, "O faithless generation, how long shall I be
with you? How long shall I bear with you? Bring him to Me." Then
they brought him to Him. And when he saw Him, immediately the
spirit convulsed him, and he fell on the ground and wallowed, foaming
at the mouth. So He asked his father, "How long has this been happening
to him?" And he said, "From childhood. And often he has thrown him
both into the fire and into the water to destroy him. But if You can do
anything, have compassion on us and help us. " Jesus said to him, "If you
can believe, all things are possible to him who believes. " Immediately
the father of the child cried out and said with tears, "Lord, I believe;
help my unbelief!" When Jesus saw that the people came running
together, He rebuked the unclean spirit, saying to it, "Deaf and dumb
spirit, I command you, come out of him and enter him no more!" Then
the spirit cried out, convulsed him greatly, and came out of him. And he
became as one dead, so that many said, "He is dead. " But Jesus took him
by the hand and lifted him up, and he arose. And when He had come
into the house, His disciples asked Him privately, "Why could we not
cast it out?" So He said to them, "This kind can come out by nothing but
prayer and fasting. "*

We learn from the above teaching that some demons require more
authority than others to be cast out. A lot of times, I have told demons
to go and they didn't. I don't feel too bad though, because the disciples
of Jesus were having the same trouble. I have learned that if I tell the
demon to leave and it doesn't then I need to break the legal right the
demon has to be in the person. The way break the legal right is by
leading the person needing deliverance to speak verbally, a properly
worded prayer of repentance. I craft a prayer and have them repeat
after me. Then I should have enough authority cast it out. If it is a deaf
and dumb spirit, I could fast and pray before the prayer session so that
I would have more authority.

I have seen people on television, often on African television, doing deliverance ministry in front of a big crowd. The demon always comes out of the person right away the first time the minister yells, "Come out!" This makes me suspect it is a fake show because it just doesn't always happen like that. When Jesus told the demons to come out of the Gadarene demoniac in Luke 8:26-30, the demons did not leave immediately. Instead, they began to negotiate with Jesus.

At one evangelistic meeting in Choma, Zambia, I was in the crowd praying for people who had responded during the altar call when I saw one of the local prayer ministers, a young man about 15 years old, casting demons out of people, one after another very quickly. I had never seen anything like it before. The authority that he had over demons was quite impressive. I stopped ministering and went to speak to the young man. I got his phone number and we had lunch the next day. He told me his testimony about how he got saved watching his father's cows. When a lightning storm came, he herded the cows under a tree to wait out the storm, but lighting struck the tree and the power of the bolt knocked him out. When he awoke, he had a saying in his head, so he went home to ask his mother what the saying was. She suggested he go to a Christian to ask them because she thought it could be something from the Bible. A Christian relative explained that it was a Bible scripture that was sovereignly put into his mind. Quite a sovereign salvation story! Along with His salvation came an incredible amount of authority over demons. I am still in contact with this man; he has graduated seminary and is now pastoring a church in Swaziland.

There is a saying in deliverance circles, "You can't cast out what you have. " I believe that is true for the most part, but self-deliverance is casting out what you have. It does seem though, that it is harder to self-deliver from the higher-level demons. I believe that demons in other people recognize which demons you have. An example of that is the victim-predator syndrome in which the demons in the predator see the demons in the victim and are attracted to them. So, it would make sense that if you have a demon and are trying to cast the same demon out of someone else, it might not respond. I recommend that all Christians get as free as possible, especially if you want to be an effective deliverance minister. Freedom is linked to authority, authority is linked to power, and faith intensifies authority. Remember Jesus' words regarding authority:

Jesus said to him, "If you can believe, all things are possible to him who believes." (Mark 9:23)

Once you begin to move with authority over evil spirits, your faith will rise up. If you believe that all things are possible through Christ, then you will expect the demons to leave when you command them to go. When I cast out demons, I expect them to leave, not caring even if someone has been diagnosed with a chemical imbalance in their brain by a medical doctor. The unclean spirit that is causing that chemical imbalance will be coming out because I believe all things are possible.

The laying on of hands can transfer the baptism of the Holy Spirit and a healing anointing. Also, I believe that it can pass on authority over evil. My own authority over evil spirts increased after having hands laid on me while receiving impartations from spiritual fathers and mothers.

CHAPTER 28
GENERATIONAL PRAYER MODEL

Generational Prayer Model [1]

S alvation is a gift from God through His grace. There is nothing we can do to earn it. Once we give our life to Christ, in addition to salvation, we regain access to the authority given up when mankind first sinned. (Genesis, Chapter 3).

Even though salvation is free, we must still work out this salvation. (Philippians 2:12). Working out salvation means following God's lead as we exercise the authority we have through Jesus Christ to clean up our lives and our family line.

Generational prayer gives us an opportunity to do this.

This model is intended as a starting point, not a method. It is imperative that we always follow God's lead.

For a more thorough explanation, and a demonstration of this model, we invite you to go to http://aslansplace. com/ and watch "Understanding Generational Prayer".

Step 1: Briefly get to know the person you are about to pray for.
Step 2: Briefly introduce self (i. e. your background, history, etc.).
Step 3: Provide a brief explanation about generational strongholds.

*"The LORD passed in front of Moses, calling out, 'Yahweh! The
LORD! The God of compassion and mercy! I am slow to anger and
filled with unfailing love and faithfulness. I lavish unfailing love to a
thousand generations. I forgive iniquity, rebellion, and sin. But I do not
excuse the guilty. I lay the sins of the parents upon their children and
grandchildren; the entire family is affected — even children in the third
and fourth generations. '"* (Exodus 34:6-7 NLT)

Step 4: Provide a brief explanation about the gift of discernment from
Hebrews 5:13:

  a. Touch (Acts 12:7)
  b. Smell (Psalm 45:8)
  c. Hearing (2 Samuel 5:22-24)
  d. Taste (Job 6:30)
  e. Sight (Isaiah 6:10)
  f. Evil default* (Acts 16:18)

Step 5: Open in prayer: Holy Spirit I invite you to cleanse (person's
name) generational line. In the name of Jesus, I command all evil to
leave (person's name) family line and go to the feet of Jesus! Amen.

Step 6: Determine the generational issue. Ask the person if they
have had:

  a. A recent or recurring dream.
  b. If they haven't, ask them if they have had a childhood
  memory of anything that has troubled them over the years.

Note: A recent or recurring dream or troubling memory will be
the starting point of the generational prayer process. For example, if the person has had a dream or memory about lust, there
is likely a stronghold of sexual impurity in their family line. If
the person remembers their childhood being very lonely, loneliness may be something the enemy planted in their family line.

Note: The Lord may give you a strategic dream the morning of your appointment that reveals the stronghold.

Step 7: Determine when the stronghold began

Ask: Lord, how many generations back was (generational issue) empowered in (person's name's) family line?

Note: The Holy Spirit will give the person you are praying for (and you) and other team members, the numbers of the specific generations when the enemy empowered evil in the person's family line. The Holy Spirit will do this by giving you an impression or vision, etc. Note: As the Holy Spirit gives different numbers when lust or loneliness was empowered and re-empowered in the generational line be cognizant of any sensory confirmation (hits in the Spirit) on your body.

Clue: The stronger the sensory confirmation, the greater the presence of evil in that particular generation.

Step 8: Determine the country

Ask: Lord, what country was (the generational issue) empowered in?

Step 9: Determine what happened

Ask: Lord, what happened (i. e. an event) at this generation to empower (i. e. lust or loneliness) in the family line?

Wait on the Lord to show you "how" the enemy infiltrated the family line.

Step 10: Start with the biggest number and ask the Holy Spirit: Lord, what happened at (such and such's) generation to empower (i. e. lust or loneliness) in the generational line?

As soon as you have prayed this prayer, "wait" on the Lord to give you a "word of knowledge," "impression" or "vision" as to what happened in this specific generation to empower the sin (i. e. lust or loneliness) in the generational line. For example, you may hear the words "prostitution", "orgies", etc.

Step 11: Then pray: In the name of Jesus I come against all evil that has been given the legal right to establish the stronghold of [lust] in (person's name) family line. I break, shatter and destroy [lust] from the (start with the generation you determined in step 7) and demand that (root of generational issue i. e. lust) go to the feet of Jesus!

Note: (Wait for the evil to leave. (We find most often that you will sense this through your discernment. Some can discern evil by feeling pressure on there head in a certain spot. This spot can be called your evil defaulton your head.)

Step 12: Have the person pray through "Renunciation of Sins in the Family Line" from Aslan's Place "Prayers for Generational Deliverance. "

Note: As the person is praying this prayer, take careful note of any impressions, sensations, visions you have. As they come to mind command them to leave (e. g. say "lust leave. " "Sexual impurity leave. " etc.). Be sure to explain that when you are telling the strongholds to leave that it does not reflect upon them personally but is the evil leaving their generational line.

Step 13: Once the person has finished renouncing the sins in their family, line go to the next lowest number of generational sin. (Remember you started with the highest number) Pray: Lord at the _th generation, what re-empowered [i. e. lust or loneliness] in the family line.

Step 14: Wait on the Lord to show you which prayer to have the person pray from Aslan's Place prayer manual. Keep in mind that the

Holy Spirit does something different in each deliverance session. Because of this you can't rely on set prayers for every session. Some of the most commonly used prayers are:

- *Prayer Breaking Ungodly Ties Between a Person and the Dimensions*
- *Prayer of Renunciation for the Misogynistic Spirit*
- *Prayer to Release One from the Ungodly Depths*
- *Prayer of Release from Chronic, Physical, Mental and Spiritual Disorders*
- *Prayer to Release Supernatural Favor to Proclaim the Favorable Year of the Lord*

Step 15: Continue on to the next lowest number and repeat the above prayer process until you come to the present generation. At this point pray: From the present generation to (person's name) descendants to a thousand generations. Next, ask the person to close their eyes and ask the following questions:

1. Can you see yourself as a creative spirit before God's throne (mention Jeremiah 1:5)?
2. Did you want to join your mother and father's sperm and egg at conception?
3. Did anything happen to you between leaving God's throne and conception?
4. Ask: Lord, did, any ungodly trades occur?
See Ezekiel 27:13 (ESV), Joel 3:3, Revelation 18:13 (ESV)

Note: Ungodly trades occur when unborn children are "dedicated" to false altars. For example, parents could dedicate their future child to an animal in the Zodiac (the snake, the dragon, etc.). Ungodly trades also occur when blood is shed.

Step 16: Ask the Lord to remove all idols and false altars from the family line.

Step 17: Have the person pray the following prayer:

> Lord, I repent for those in my family line who traded human souls with the enemy for present favor. I repent for this and I demand back from the enemy all parts of my spirit, soul and body that were scattered. I declare to my spirit, soul and body that I will yield to the Holy Spirit. I repent for all blood sacrifices and offerings of blood in my family line that gave the enemy the legal right to scatter parts of my spirit, soul and body among the ungodly stars. I now, declare that I will rule and reign over the gates and doors assigned to me and my family line! Please remove all evil that tried to prevent me from being conceived. Amen!

Step 18: Have the person pray the prayer, *Ruling and Reigning with Christ*.

Step 19: Follow the *Rapid Healing Model* in the *Prayers for Generational Deliverance*.

Step 20: Conclude the prayer session by blessing the person by speaking Numbers 6:24-27 and Isaiah 11:2-3 over their life:

> May the Lord bless you with many gifts! May the Lord guard you with a hedge of protection! May the Lord illuminate the wholeness of His being toward you to bring order to your life! May the Lord beautify you! May the Lord lift up His wholeness of being and look upon you and set in place all you need to be whole and complete! May the Spirit of the Lord rest on you! May the Spirit of wisdom and understanding guide you! May the Spirit of counsel and might move mightily through you! And may the Spirit of knowledge and the fear of the Lord encounter you at all times. In Jesus' name, Amen.

CHAPTER 29
CONCLUSION

Through these simple biblical principles, I have been able to help lead many people into greater levels of freedom and healing. Also, as I have shared, several prayer ministers have helped my wife and me enter into a freedom that we never dreamed possible. Though I faithfully attended a Charismatic church that believed evil spirits could be in Christians, little was ever taught about it for seventeen years. Our pastors would talk about the devil but never go into details, partly because they didn't want to scare people out of the church and partly because they didn't have the understanding or revelation about how deliverance actually works.

Through the loving and compassionate ministry of a few people, I can now say that I feel God's peace, the peace that surpasses understanding. My wife Anne and I are a walking testimony of how a marriage that was in a struggle to survive has changed into a wonderful relationship that we both enjoy. Living together without the inevitable arguments allows us to get to know each other fully. Consequently, a rich trust and understanding has blossomed between us. Absolutely, it is what I always wanted but had never been able to achieve; there just wasn't anyone we knew who could help us understand the simple fact that the demons in both of us were the problem. With them out of the picture, life is so much better; there is truly peace, revelation, and His power working through us.

Jesus rejoiced in the Spirit, saying:

I thank You, Father, Lord of heaven and earth, that You have hidden these things from the wise and prudent and revealed them to babes. Even so, Father, for so it seemed good in Your sight. (Matthew 25-26)

The way deliverance ministry works is sometimes hidden, but God reveals it to those whom He chooses. You may be one of the 'babes' that He reveals it to, thus enabling you to be one who becomes a worker of miracles. Such a ministry does not come without a cost. Deliverance ministers are often misunderstood in the church and usually do not receive many accolades. They may easily be deemed 'kooks' or witches, slandered by mouth or on social media. They work behind the scenes, laboring in prayer, helping others to the best of their ability and gifting, grieving at just how bad people are hurting until they are willing to come to Jesus for help. There is a burden that comes with knowing that help is available, but many people refuse to come humbly before Jesus to ask for help.

In contrast, there is a very deep satisfaction in seeing someone that you ministered to who had been so tormented, now walking in victory, worshiping God in freedom and truth. I saw one such lady in church one day, and she gave me a hug—it was a wonderful feeling. What had been given to me, I was able to give to another. Deliverance is truly a ministry of compassion.

I will close with another quote from Jesus:

And as you go, preach, saying, 'The kingdom of heaven is at hand. Heal the sick, cleanse the lepers, raise the dead, cast out demons. Freely you have received, freely give. (Matthew 10:7-8)

ABOUT THE AUTHOR

Josef Rousek is CEO of Mt. Whitney Coffee Roasters in Bishop, California and Vice President of Father's Heart Africa. He is a businessman, entrepreneur, evangelist, prayer minister, and has shared the Gospel of Jesus Christ in Zambia, Zimbabwe, and in nations around the world. He graduated from Aslan's Leadership Academy, a Biblical training and equipping center, founded by Dr. Paul Cox. Josef and his wife, Anne, reside in High Sierra Mountains of California.

For more information:
https://www.facebook.com/Fathers.Heart.Africa/
deliverancecompassion@gmail.com

VIDEOS

BY JOSEF ROUSEK

Deliverance Part 1:
A Ministry of Compassion
https://youtu.be/8bOMlIgKMbo

Deliverance Part 2:
How Josef realized he was bound by demons
https://youtu.be/ZXXho_Vblrg

Deliverance Part 3:
Demons, what are they and where do they come from?
https://youtu.be/qSDz7N2jpyM

Deliverance Part 4:
Demon spirit have certain characteristics
https://youtu.be/Kt82CxIhGEE

Deliverance Part 5:
Demons, disembodied spirits or fallen angels?
https://youtu.be/SJ4-sxnTdsM

THANK YOU

Thank you for reading *Deliverance: The Ministry of Compassion.* This is our first book for all generations, bringing encouragement, walking in victory, and worshiping God in freedom and truth. Deliverance is truly a ministry of compassion.

Please visit our Facebook page at Father's Heart Africa for updates, events, support, and encouragement. Check out the Videos page, where I share key insights in the Word of God, and personal testimonies. Share with a friend!

If interested, contact me for more resources, upcoming conferences, or ministry equipping and training workshops at deliverancecompassion@gmail.com. Receive additional devotional tips and resources.

Exploring Heavenly Places Volume I:
Investigating Dimensions of Healing (10 Book Series)
by Paul L. Cox and Barbara Kain Parker

In this introductory book, we have included articles regarding aspects of the body, soul and spirit in order to provide a basic understanding of these elements of our humanity and help us see how our beings interact with the unseen. The shattering of these aspects of our lives through wounding prohibits us from becoming all that the Lord wants us to be, and enables the enemy to profit from what is rightfully ours. The cure for this pain will be further explored throughout the book series, Exploring Heavenly Places. Exploring Heavenly Places is a new book series that will explore the amazing and complex world of the spiritual heavenly places that affect our physical world.

Available in paperback and eBook
Available on Amazon

Come Up Higher
by Paul L. Cox

People are hungry for greater spiritual freedom in their life. In our ministry at Aslan's Place we've seen this evidenced in hundreds of requests for our manual, *Prayers for Generational Deliverance*. God has used these prayers to bring remarkable freedom to people. Explore the biblical, theological, and historical settings of forty-two prayers that God has used to impact lives. Discover more of the freedom God through prayers.

Available in paperback, hardback, and eBook
Available on Amazon

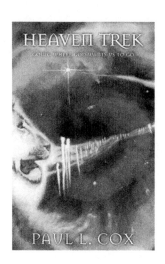

Heaven Trek: Daring to go Where God Wants Us to Go
by Paul L. Cox

The Lord now invites you to "Boldly Go Where Man Has Never Gone Before!" It is an adventure into the unknown. This is not Christianity as usual. Are you ready for the adventure? Are you ready to travel to new realms of His glorious creation? you are welcomed aboard for His Heaven Trek.

Available in paperback and eBook
Available on Amazon

They Shall Expel Demons
by Derek Prince

WHAT ARE DEMONS? HOW DO DEMONS GAIN ENTRY? DO CHRISTIANS EVER NEED DELIVER-ANCE? In this book, Derek Prince answers many vital questions. Are you struggling with problems that never go away? Has it ever occurred to you that demons may be at work? Perhaps you want to help others. *"Jesus never sent anyone out to preach the Gospel without instructing and equipping them to take action against demons."*

Available in paperback and eBook
Available on Amazon

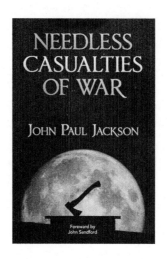

Needless Casualties of War
by John Paul Jackson

Timeless Classic: Essential must-read! Prayer is a powerful weapon, a two-edged sword, not to be wielded carelessly. Although we have authority as the children of God, how we fight can determine our personal consequences in the battle of the millennium. In this timely book, John Paul Jackson reveals some startling insights that will uncover spiritual strategies of the dark side. Find out how you can protect yourself from Satan's onslaught and escape his unforeseen and unperceived attacks. Endorsed and highly recommended by R.T. Kendall!

Available in paperback and eBook
Available on Amazon

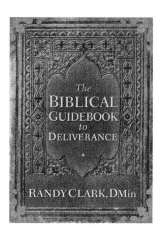

The Biblical Guidebook to Deliverance
by Randy Clark

Many people are unconsciously living in bondage. Marriages are failing, drugs are rampant, pornography is everywhere, and evenChristians have given up—on God, the church, and themselves.

The Biblical Guidebook to Deliverance provides you with the supernatural power and authority to fight your battles and be free from oppression. Full of scriptural, yet practical, teaching this book will help you learn how deliverance was part of Jesus's ministry in the New Testament, and how you have access to the same power—enabling you to live free from the chains of sin.

No matter what situation you are going through, God will give you His grace so that you can rejoice in freedom and live in the fullness of life that He intends for you.

Available in paperback book and eBook
Available on Amazon

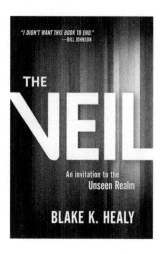

The Veil: An Invitation to the Unseen Realm
by Blake Healy

For as long as he can remember, Blake K. Healy has seen angels and demons. He sees them as clearly as he would see you if you were standing right in front of him. He sees angels dancing in worship services and whispering words of encouragement in people's ears. He also sees demons latching on to people and perpetuating addiction and bitterness in their hearts.

The Veil chronicles how Blake matured in this gifting, while overcoming the fear and confusion of what he saw, how he learned to use his gift of seeing for God's glory, and how to teach others to do the same.

This new and updated version of *The Veil* also includes a brief guide on how to begin growing in the gift of seeing in the spirit yourself, as well as an appendix of scriptural references to the spirit realm and angels, along with Blake's commentary on these passages.

Available in paperback, audio, and eBook
Available on Amazon

PROFOUND GOOD
See God Through the Lens of His Love

BLAKE K. HEALY

Profound Good: See God Through the Lens of His Love
by Blake Healy

What you see of God is only part of the story.
From the time Blake Healy was a small child, he has seen angels,
demons, and other spiritual things. He sees them with his naked eyes,
as vividly and clearly as anything else. Everyplace he goes, every person
he meets, every day that goes by, he sees in the spirit. After thirty years
of seeing in the spirit, one thing has consistently been the most painful
for him to see. It is not when he sees someone trapped in demonic
oppression. It is not when he sees the gaping wounds of emotional
trauma. It is when he sees the goodness of God go unclaimed by His
people. In this book, Healy takes readers on a journey of rediscovering
the goodness of God. It fills the churches.. It moves across the sea
from nation to nation. Learn how to see it and receive it, and then
watch every corner of the world be completely transformed by the
power of His profound good.

Available in paperback, audio, and eBook
Available on Amazon

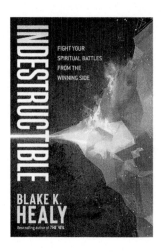

Indestructible: Fight Your Spiritual Battles From the Winning Side
by Blake Healy

This book will teach you how to battle your spiritual struggles from the winning side so that you can be victorious both in your life and in the issues happening in today's world. Many Christians limp through their lives feeling beat up by the enemy, their circumstances, and internal strife. They look at the pattern of world events with a sense of hopelessness. Too often they simply accept these as the natural trials and challenges of life. However, other Christians acknowledge that there is a war happening, a battle between angels and demons. They want to know: What are the rules of engagement for this battle? What weapons do we have? What kind of enemy are we facing? Is this battle always happening, or are there moments of rest and peace? Am I really meant to fight in a battle where I can't see my enemies or my allies? *Indestructible* will show readers how to have complete victory in their daily spiritual battles and join the front lines as heaven invades earth.

Available in paperback and eBook
Available on Amazon

NOTES

2. EVANGELISTIC MEETINGS

1. John 6:44, 15:26, 16:13-14
2. Philippians 1:6
3. Luke 8:30

6. WHAT ARE DEMONS?

1. https://www. gotquestions. org/pre-Adamic-race. html
2. http://www. khouse. org/articles/1997/110/
3. George H. Pember, *Earth's Earliest Ages* (Crane, MO: Defender, 2012) 175-176.
4. Deuteronomy 3:11

8. DO DEMONS AFFLICT CHRISTIANS?

1. Randy Clark, *The Biblical Guidebook to Deliverance*, Charisma House, c. 2015

9. BODY, SOUL AND SPIRIT

1. Colossians 2:13
2. Galatians 3:13; Ephesians 1:7;
3. Ephesians 2:6
4. Ephesians 1:13
5. https://www. ministrysamples. org/excerpts/THE-SOUL-HAVING-THREE-PARTS. HTML
6. Cox, Paul L & Parker, Barbara Kain, *Exploring Heavenly Places, Volume I: Investigating Dimensions of Healing* (Apple Valley, CA: Aslan's Place Publications, p. 31).

11. PERSONAL SIN

1. https://www. medicaldaily. com/tattoos-affect-your-health-long-term-side-effects-ink-has-your-immune-system-404404

12. OCCULT PRACTICES

1. Thomas Horn, *Zenith 2016* , Defender , Crane Missouri 65633, 2013) 180
2. https://en. wikipedia. org/wiki/Ouija

13. THE UNGODLY POWER OF WORDS

1. Matthew 18:18
2. Matthew 12:36-37
3. http://aslansplace.   com/language/en/prayer-of-release-for-masons-and-their-descendants/

14. ADDICTIONS

1. https://www. barna. com/the-porn-phenomenon/
2. https://biblehub. com/greek/5331. htm
3. https://www. merriam-webster. com/dictionary/debauchery
4. https://www.   foxnews.   com/us/south-carolina-woman-who-gouged-her-eyes-out-thought-it-was-a-sacrifice-to-god

15. AT THE HANDS OF OTHERS

1. Randy Clark, *The Biblical Guidebook to Deliverance ,Randy Clark 2015*
2. Derick Prince, *They Shall Expel Demons* Grand Rapids, MI: Chosen Books, 1998) 100

16. SEX & DEMONIZATION

1. *Women Absorb And Retain DNA From Every Man They Have Sex With,* (Baxter Dmitry Health: June 23, 2017) 362
2. Peter Horrobin, *Healing Through Deliverance* Grand Rapids, MI: Chosen Books, 2008
3. https://www. christian-faith. com/out-of-mormon-deception/
4. http://aslansplace.   com/language/en/prayer-to-break-all-ties-to-the-incubus-and-succubus-spirits/
5. Peter Horrobin, *Healing Through Deliverance*Grand Rapids, MI: Chosen Books, 2008
6. https://en. wiktionary. org/wiki/transvestite
7. https://www. merriam-webster. com/dictionary/transsexual

17. THE UNDEFILED MARRIAGE BED

1. https://biblehub. com/greek/5446. htm

18. SEXUAL RESPONSIBILITY IN MARRIAGE

1. Linda Dillow and Lorraine Pintus, *Intimate Issues,* Water Brook Press, Colorado Springs 1999

19. THE DECEIVED CHURCH

1. Philippians 2:12

22. 'GETTING ONTO IT'

1. https://biblehub. com/greek/2659. htm

25. GENERATIONAL CURSES

1. Cox, Paul L, *Come Up Higher,* (Libertyville, IL, This Joy Books, 2010), p. 79-82

28. GENERATIONAL PRAYER MODEL

1. Used with permission. For more information and links to prayers, please refer to http://aslansplace.com/

The prayers provided on this website have been developed during bible studies, prayer sessions and through revelation. We have faith that they have been provided by God, and we test them all against God's Holy Word. These prayers are not a quick fix. Instead, they are starting points as you work out your freedom in Christ. Be ready to adjust these prayers as you and those you pray with listen to the Holy Spirit. Permission is given to reproduce this prayer in its entirety provided that no changes are made. In addition, please reference Aslan's Place and www.aslansplace.com on all reproductions.

This model is included in our book Prayers for Generational Deliverance.

Printed in Great Britain
by Amazon

80365798R00119